W R I G H T S L A W

All About
Tests and Assessments

Answers to Frequently Asked Questions

Melissa Lee Farrall, Ph.D., SAIF
Pamela Darr Wright, MA, MSW
Peter W. D. Wright, Esq.

Harbor House Law Press, Inc.
Hartfield, Virginia 23071

Wrightslaw: All About Tests and Assessments
by Melissa Lee Farrall, Pamela Darr Wright, and Peter W. D. Wright

Library of Congress Cataloging-in-Publication Data
Farrall, Melissa Lee, Pamela Darr Wright and Peter W.D. Wright
Wrightslaw: All About Tests and Assessments, 1st edition
p. cm.
Includes bibliographic references and index.
ISBN 13: 978-1-892320-23-0
1. Psychological tests for children — I. Title
2. Special education — parent participation — United States.
Library of Congress Control Number: 2014900774

10 9 8 7 6 5 4 3 2 1

Printing History

Harbor House Law Press, Inc. issues new printings and new editions to keep our publications current. New printings include technical corrections and minor changes. New editions include major revisions of text and/or changes.
First Edition: May 2014

Disclaimer

The purpose of this book is to educate and inform. While the Publisher attempted to ensure that this book is accurate, there may be mistakes, typographical and in content. The authors and Publisher shall have no liability nor responsibility with respect to loss or damage alleged to be caused by information contained in this book. Every effort was made to ensure that no copyrighted material was used without permission.

When You Use a Self-Help Book

The information contained in this book is general information and may or may not reflect current developments. Tests are included in this book for a variety of reasons. Inclusion is not necessarily a recommendation, and does not mean that a test is appropriate for your child. Consult with your evaluator and your team for more information. For legal advice about a specific set of facts, consult with an attorney.

Bulk Purchases

Harbor House Law Press books are available at half price discounts for bulk purchases, academic sales or textbook adoptions. For information, contact Harbor House Law Press, P. O. Box 480, Hartfield VA 23071. Please provide the title of the book, ISBN number, quantity, how the book will be used, and date needed. Toll Free Phone Orders: (877) LAW IDEA or (877) 529-4332. Toll Free Fax Orders: (800) 863-5348. Internet Orders: orders@ harborhouselaw.com

Acknowledgements

We wish to acknowledge the contributions of several individuals who provided ideas and assistance with this book.

We want to express our gratitude to **Leeanne Seaver**, an expert on educational advocacy and family support. As Leeanne read and edited, she provided the energy and encouragement we needed to restart and finish this book.

We thank **Dr. Boris Gindis** of the Center for Cognitive-Developmental Assessment and Remediation in New York and Phoenix. Dr. Gindis specializes in working with children who are international adoptees. He offers invaluable services to children, parents, educators, and to those of us who are trying to write books.

John O. Willis, Ed.D., SAIF, Senior Lecturer in Education, Rivier University; Assessment Specialist, Regional Services and Education Center, Amherst, New Hampshire, assisted us with his exceptional expertise in assessment. As always, he delivered his critiques with humor and kindness. The adjectives in the thesaurus under headings of greatest, expert, and brilliant fail do to him justice.

We owe special thank you to **Deborah Mullan** for her efforts to improve our writing. She has an unparalleled eye for detail in content and in form.

Many people selflessly gave their time to review portions of **Wrightslaw: All About Tests and Assessments**. We want to thank you for reading and critiquing sections of the manuscript.

Loni Allen, Advocacy trainer and parent of children with disabilities. Education Specialist, Parents Helping Parents, PTIC in California.

Marilyn Bartlett, J.D., Ph.D., Professor of Educational Law and Policy at Texas A&M University in Kingsville and Special Education Advocate in Manatee-Sarasota Counties, Florida.

Betsy Moog Brooks, M.S., CED, LSLS Cert. AVEd, Executive Director, The Moog Center for Deaf Education, St. Louis, Missouri.

Pam Cook, M.Ed., Advocate, ABC Consulting Services, Pittsburgh, Pennsylvania.

Sue Davis-Killian, Education Advocate, Gold Coast Down Syndrome Organization, Palm Beach County, Florida.

Harry L. Gewanter, M.D., FAAP, FACR, Pediatrician for and parent of children with disabilities, Richmond, Virginia.

Pat Howey, Advocate from Indiana.

Natalie Hoxie, MA, BCBA, Parent of 3 children with disabilities, Board Certified Behavior Analyst, clinical supervisor for in-home behavioral services, Board of Directors Autism Society, San Diego, California.

Jackie Igafo-Te'o, Parent of two children with disabilities, and website/data consultant for disability-related organizations.

Melinda S. Jeffries, M.A., State & Federal Programs Coordinator, Beaverton Rural Schools, Michigan.

Joyce A. Kubik, ADHD coach, Certified Master Coach; Owner, Bridges to Success, President, ADHD Coaches Organization.

Debbie Larson, Parent of adult child with autism and special education advocate, Batavia, New York.

Treva Maitland, M.S., Advocate & Secondary Transition Trainer & Technical Assistance provider for The Arc Tennessee and parent of twins with disabilities.

Nagle Moussa, President National Autism Association of North Texas, Texas Education Agency Continuing Advisory Committee member, and Child and Family Advocate.

Chuck Noe, Education Specialist for Partners Resource Network, the TX Parent Training & Information (PTI) Center, retired Texas special education director.

Caryl A. Patten, New Hampshire Special Education Advocacy Center.

Penelope F. Petzold, Esq., Parent Advisor for SpEd Connecticut and advocate for her three children with learning disabilities.

Karen Putz, Parent of three deaf and hard of hearing children, Chicago, Illinois.

William B. Reichhardt, Esq., Attorney who represents parents, children, and young adults in issues related to special education and mental health in Fairfax, Virginia.

Patty Roberts, Esq., Director of William & Mary Law School's PELE Special Education Advocacy Clinic, Williamsburg, Virginia.

Kelli Sandman-Hurley, Ed.D., Co-founder, Dyslexia Training Institute, San Diego, California.

Sue Nelson Sargeant, M.S., Preschool Speech-Language Pathologist, Spotsylvania County Public Schools, Virginia.

Chan Stroman, Research Director, ParSEC Wisconsin, Madison, Wisconsin.

Kristin Tassin, Parent of a daughter with Down syndrome, Co-founder of Father's Joy, and attorney with Dry & Tassin, PLLC, Missouri City, Texas.

Mary K. Tran, Founder of LetsPlayOC.com, parent of child with autism, Orange County, California.

Lori Wathen, Parent of a child with Down syndrome, Norman, Oklahoma.

Suzanne Whitney, Special Education Advocate, Research Editor at Wrightslaw, author of the Doing Your Homework column, and co-author of ***Wrightslaw: No Child Left Behind,*** New Hampshire.

Diane Willcutts, Advocate with Education Advocacy, LLC, in West Hartford, Connecticut.

Dedication

Melissa dedicates this book to my mother and grandmother, women who used their intelligence and strength to make the world a better place for their children. I can only hope that I have done the same.

Pete dedicates this book to Diana Hanbury King, who tutored me every day for two years. I am deeply grateful to Diana who taught me to read, write, spell, and do arithmetic.

Pam dedicates this book to my friend, Sue O., for your patience, encouragement, and hard work when the road was rocky. Without you, this book would never have been published.

Table of Contents

Table of Questions

- How can I request an evaluation for special education?

- When I ask the school to evaluate my child, what information should I provide?

- Can the school decide what areas they will test?

- Must I give written consent before the school can evaluate my child?

- I wrote a letter to request an evaluation for special education and included my informed consent statement. The school says I have to sign their legal consent form. What does the law say?

- What happens if I don't give my consent for the school to evaluate my child?

- How long does the school have to evaluate and determine if my child is eligible for special education services?

- Is the school required to observe my child in the classroom?

- What happens during a classroom observation?

- The school is evaluating my child for a learning disability. A psychologist observed him during Physical Education (PE). Shouldn't the psychologist observe him in the classroom?

- My child's evaluation included computer-generated reports. Are these reports as accurate as reports written by an examiner?

- My child's psychological evaluation report did not include recommendations. Shouldn't an evaluation report by a school psychologist include recommendations?

- The school evaluated my child. I don't agree with their findings or their recommendations. What can I do?

- We obtained a comprehensive evaluation of our child by a psychologist in the private sector. We provided the evaluation to our child's IEP team. The team said they considered the evaluation and decided not to use any information or recommendations from it. Can they do that?

- Can I request a copy of the school's evaluation report before an eligibility meeting?

- My child was found eligible for special education. What happens next?

| 3 | Making Sense of Your Child's Test Scores |

- What are norm-referenced tests?

- What are criterion-referenced tests?

- What are the differences between norm-referenced and criterion-referenced tests?

- What is the Mean?

- What are Standard Deviations?

- What are raw scores?

- What are standard scores?

- What are scaled scores?

- What are T scores?

- My child has Down syndrome. The school will not provide speech and language therapy and occupational therapy because his IQ is low. Can a school refuse to provide services because a child's has a low IQ score?

- When is a score on an intelligence test invalid?

- My child is deaf and uses sign language. We want to understand his cognitive abilities. What do we need to know about evaluating a child who is deaf?

- The school wants to do an informal reading assessment on my child. What is an informal reading assessment?

- The school wants to do a screening test of my child's reading. What is a screening test?

- Who can evaluate my child's reading skills?

- Is it possible to test for dyslexia?

- My first grader's scores on the reading subtests of the Woodcock Johnson III Tests of Achievement were below average. His teacher says he will read when he is ready. Do reading test scores improve when a child matures?

- On the *Woodcock-Johnson III*, my child scored much higher on the Letter & Word Identification subtest than on the Word Attack subtest. What do these scores mean?

- My child is in second grade but he hasn't learned to read. His score on the Passage Comprehension subtest of the *Woodcock-Johnson III* was in the average range. How can he get an average score when he can't read?

- My daughter reads slowly and inaccurately. On the *Gray Oral Reading Tests, Fifth Edition* (GORT-5), her Comprehension score was average, but her fluency was well below average. I'm confused. Her reading skills are not average. How could she earn an average score?

- My son is in the first grade. He struggles to read. How can his scores on the *Standardized Reading Inventory, Second Edition*, be in the average range?

- My child has an IQ of 75 (fifth percentile). On reading tests, he earned scores in the 70s. His team says that is the best we can expect. Is this true?

- My child has autism. What do we need to know about evaluating his reading?

- My child is nonverbal. Can his reading be assessed?

- My daughter has a history of ear infections and language delays. She is struggling to learn the alphabet. Should I have her tested?

- My child's teacher said that his high scores on the *WJ-III* Basic Reading subtests mean that he has hyperlexia. What is hyperlexia? How is hyperlexia assessed?

7 Writing and Spelling Assessments

- My child struggles with writing and spelling. He needs to be evaluated. What should an assessment of written language include?

- My child has struggled with writing since first grade. Are there risk factors for problems with written expression?

- When should we have our child evaluated for written language problems?

- My child's written work is full of spelling errors. What causes spelling problems? Can her spelling problems be assessed?

- How is spelling assessed?

- Are there tests of handwriting?

- My child's handwriting is illegible. How is handwriting assessed?

- After my child had a written language assessment, the evaluator recommended that he have a speech and language evaluation. What is the connection?

- My son has weak oral language skills. He does not easily communicate what he wants to say. His expressive language scores are below average. He has difficulty writing sentences. Will his scores be low on writing tests, too?

- What is dysgraphia?

- My child struggles with reading and writing. Her scores on the *WIAT-III* Reading Comprehension test were very low so I asked the team to assess her writing. The team declined, and said there was no need. What should I do?

- My daughter is failing several classes in high school. The quality of her writing is poor. When she was tested on the *Woodcock-Johnson III Tests of Achievement*, her Broad Written Language Composite scores was in the average range. I'm confused.

- My son was tested on the *Test of Written Language, Third Edition* (TOWL-3) and later on the Fourth Edition (TOWL-4). His scores on the TOWL-4 indicated that his skills improved but we see no improvement in his writing. How can this be?

- My child's first grade teacher reports that he is having trouble learning to write. He scored in the average range on the *WJ-III* Writing Samples subtest. An average score seems high to me, considering his difficulties.

- On a spelling test, my child wrote neatly and scored in the average range. On a test that required him to write a story, his handwriting was messy and his spelling was poor. Does he need help with writing?

- My child has poor handwriting and was evaluated by Occupational Therapist at school. The OT used the *Beery Buktenica Developmental Test of Visual-Motor Integration, Fifth Edition* (VMI5). My child earned an average score. The OT said my child could write neatly if he tried harder. Is this correct? Does the VMI5 test handwriting?

- My child's written work is full of spelling errors. I don't know if her problems are caused by a disability or lack of teaching. Can I request that the school evaluate her spelling?

8   Mathematics and Math Assessments

- The school plans to evaluate my child for a math disability. What should a math evaluation include?

- My daughter says she hates math. Math does not come easily to her but I think she can learn if she works at it. Should we get a math assessment?

- My first grader is struggling to learn math. When can a child be evaluated to determine if he has a learning disability in math?

- What is dyscalculia?

- What role does memory play in difficulties with math?

- How is working memory assessed?

- My child spends hours on math homework but he's failing math. His score on a math fluency subtest was far below average. Does he have a learning disability in math?

- One of my students is having difficulty learning fractions. Can we test for this problem?

- My fourth grader struggles with basic number sense. Are there programs that help kids who are struggling in math?

- My daughter is a poor reader. She is scheduled to take the *WIAT-III* Math Problem Solving subtest. Can the teacher read this test to her?

- My daughter has high functioning autism and a learning disability in math. Can you recommend tests to measure her working memory and math skills?

- My 11 year old skips numbers and puts them in the wrong places. He doesn't seem to know whether to add or subtract or what the signs mean. Is this because he has ADHD? Should we have him tested for a math disability?

- My son is bright, talkative, and friendly but he is failing in math and English composition. The school plans to evaluate him. What do we need to know?

- My daughter is diagnosed with dyslexia. She enters middle school this year, but does not know her math facts. What should we do?

9 Speech and Language Assessments

- My child has speech and language problems. Friends and family often cannot understand what he says. What do I need to know about speech and language assessments?

- Who administers speech and language evaluations?

- My four-year old's speech is delayed. How can I tell if he has a language problem or is just a "late-bloomer"?

- How will the evaluator assess my child's receptive language skills?

- How will the evaluator assess my child's expressive language skills?

- My child has difficulty expressing his thoughts. His scores were in the average range on the *WIAT-III* Oral Expression subtest. The school says he doesn't need help. I do not agree.

- When my daughter speaks, she often has to stop to "find" the next word. How can this problem be assessed?

- On the PPVT-5, my child earned a very high score when asked to point to pictures of words. On the EVT-2, he earned a very low score when asked to name pictures and provide synonyms. Which score should we rely on?

- My first grader's speech is soft and difficult to understand. Is he too young to be tested?

- What should an evaluation of articulation and phonological disorders include?

- My child stutters. His classmates tease him. His teacher says he will grow out of it. How long do we have to wait?

- My child's speech is choppy and hard to understand. He understands language better than he can speak. His doctor thinks he may have childhood apraxia of speech. What is apraxia of speech? Should he have a speech and language evaluation?

- What tests should be included in an evaluation for childhood apraxia of speech?

- My child has autism. The evaluator said he has weaknesses in pragmatics. What are pragmatics?

- How are pragmatics evaluated?

- My three-year-old is being evaluated for autism. His ability to communicate is limited. The evaluation includes a speech and language assessment. What should we expect from this assessment?

- My child's teacher says his language usage is "concrete." What does this mean?

- My daughter has a nonverbal learning disability and often misunderstands what people say. After the school tested her with the *Clinical Evaluation of Language Fundamentals, Fifth Edition* (CELF-5), they said she does not qualify for speech services. I don't get it.

10 Evaluations for Learning Disabilities and Attention-Deficit/Hyperactivity Disorders

- My son is bright but has always struggled to learn in school. In most subjects, his grades are poor. Should I have him evaluated for a learning disability?

- What should be included in an evaluation for a specific learning disability?

- How can I prepare for my child's evaluation?

- What information is included in the evaluation report?

- When I met with the school team, they said they had to do a classroom observation. Is this right?

- Who is qualified to diagnose specific learning disabilities?

- A psychologist evaluated my child and diagnosed him with dyslexia. The school team said dyslexia is not a qualifying disability so they will not provide services. What should I do?

- The school evaluations show that my child has a learning disability. What can I do to help my child learn and catch up?

- My child has ADHD. He is very active and has difficulty staying on a task. Can he be tested?

- My daughter has ADHD. Our doctor advised us to request special education from her school. The school said she is not eligible for special education because she makes passing grades. Now what?

- Can a child with a disability who receives passing grades and is passing from grade to grade be eligible for special education?

- My child has ADHD. His teachers say he is smart but his scores on the IQ test were low. What happened?

- My son has so much energy. He fidgets and is out of his seat in class. He has a short attention span and a poor memory. Could he have ADHD?

- What are executive functioning skills?

- What tests are used to measure executive functioning skills?

- A clinical psychologist diagnosed my child with an executive functioning disorder. The school team says he is not eligible for special education. Is this true?

- My child is in RTI. He is not making progress. The school will not refer him for a special education evaluation until he stays in RTI for several months. Is this legal?

- One of my students was diagnosed with dyslexia in first grade. He has been receiving RTI for over a year with no evidence of progress. The team refuses to evaluate him. What can I do?

 11   Assessments of Hearing, Vision, and Motor Skills

- When should I have my child screened for hearing problems?

- My child is scheduled for a hearing assessment. What should we expect?

- The audiologist told me our daughter has a mild-to-moderate hearing loss. Should we be concerned?

- My child will have a comprehensive special education evaluation. He has a severe hearing loss. How should we prepare for this evaluation?

- My child has a hearing impairment and communication problems. Will the evaluator understand him?

- After the school screened my child's vision, they recommended that she have a comprehensive vision examination. What should I know about vision examinations?

- My child has pediatric glaucoma with severe vision loss. The school wants to evaluate her for special education services. What should we know about this evaluation?

- My daughter is blind. The school wants to administer an IQ test that is not designed for blind children. Can I ask the school not to use this IQ test?

- I teach children who are visually impaired. What should I know about assessing children who have significant visual impairments?

- My child has cerebral palsy. He is being evaluated for special education. What do I need to know about the evaluation?

- My child has spinal bifida and needs physical therapy(PT). When I asked the team to add physical therapy to her IEP, they scheduled a physical therapy evaluation. What should I know about PT evaluations?

- Who does physical therapy evaluations?

- How can an occupational therapist help?

- My child has learning disabilities and an IEP. He has fine motor deficits. His handwriting is illegible. He has difficulty getting organized and completing homework assignments. Can I ask the school to provide help with handwriting and organizational skills?

- My child has autism and does not speak. He needs a communication system.

12 Auditory, Visual, Visual-Motor, and Sensory Processing Assessments

- My daughter has difficulty remembering and following directions. Her doctor says she needs to be assessed for an auditory processing assessment. What is an auditory processing disorder?

- Who evaluates auditory processing disorders in children?

- My child has frequent ear infections. Can ear infections cause an auditory processing disorder?

- My child has 20/20 vision but the teacher says she struggles with visual processing.

- How is visual processing assessed?

- My child was diagnosed with dyspraxia. What is dyspraxia?

- How does dyspraxia affect my child's ability to learn?

- Who can evaluate a child for dyspraxia?

- What should I know about my child's evaluation for dyspraxia?

- My son was evaluated with the *Rey Osterrieth Complex Figure Test* that required him to copy a design. The evaluator said he is "disorganized." What does this mean?

- My child is scheduled for a sensory processing evaluation. What should I know about this evaluation?

- Who conducts sensory processing evaluations?

13 Assessment of Adaptive Behavior and Behavior

- What is an adaptive behavior assessment?

- Who does adaptive behavior assessments?

- Is there one good test that measures adaptive behavior?

- The school used the *Vineland Adaptive Behavior Scales, Second Edition* as part of my daughter's assessment. I asked for the parent/caregiver form. The team said only the teacher fills out a form. Is this correct?

- How can I prepare for my child's adaptive behavior assessment?

- What is a functional behavior assessment (FBA)?

- Who can do functional behavior assessments?

- Shouldn't bad behaviors be punished?

- What do behavior specialists look for when conducting an FBA?

14 Transition Assessments

- What are transition assessments? How are these assessments used?

- How old should my daughter be when we start the transition assessment process?

- Who conducts transition assessments?

- As a parent, do I have a role to play in the transition assessment process?

- What tests should be included in my child's transition assessment?

- My child does not read. Can any transition assessments be used with non-readers?

- The school team does not want to do a transition assessment on my child because she severely handicapped. What should I do?

- Who are English Language Learners?

- Who evaluates English Language Learners (ELLs)?

- Should an evaluator assess an English Language Learner in her native language or with tests in English?

- My child is learning English (ELL). She is struggling in school. Could she have a language learning disorder?

- A school psychologist evaluated our ELL daughter. The intelligence test included tests of vocabulary and verbal reasoning. He said her IQ was low. We disagree. What should we do?

- I teach in a district with many ELL children. Their parents have limited skills in English. What are our responsibilities to parents who attend IEP meetings but do not understand English?

- The administrators at my child's school say they do not have access to interpreters. Are there resources that provide interpreters?

- Few tests are available to measure the skills of ELLs. Can an evaluator use tests that were standardized on English-speaking children?

- Why can't normed, standardized tests be translated into other languages?

- My child is learning to speak English. She did not learn to read well in Spanish. I worry that she will have trouble learning to read in English.

- How do multicultural factors affect testing?

- How does bilingualism affect the evaluations of an ELL?

- What should an evaluation of an internationally adopted (IA) child from an institution include?

- We adopted a child from an orphanage in China. The school says we should defer testing until our child settles in and learns some English. Is this correct?

- We adopted a child from an orphanage in Russia. The school psychologist who will evaluate our child is not a bilingual specialist. He wants a person who speaks Russian to assist with the assessment. Is this a good idea?

- We adopted our child from Poland a year ago. He does not remember Polish. English is his only language. The school insists on a bilingual assessment. What should we do?

Introduction

- What is in This Book?

- Who Should Read This Book?

- How This Book is Organized

- How to Use This Book

If your child is struggling in school, you need to find out why. If you are concerned about your child's learning, academic progress, social skills, or behavior, a comprehensive assessment will identify the nature of his problems and help you develop a plan.

If your child has a disability, you need objective information about his strengths, weaknesses, and needs before making decisions about his educational program. You will find this information in the tests and assessments completed on your child.

If you are like most people, you have questions about tests. How do tests measure skills? What do the test scores mean? Should you request specific tests?

All About Tests and Assessments

You will find answers to many of your questions in *Wrightslaw: All About Tests and Assessments*. Some answers may surprise you.

"My third grader struggles to read. His grades have dropped. The school is threatening to retain him. Does he have a learning disability?"

"When the school tested my child with an intelligence test, he earned an IQ score of 65 (1st percentile). His team says that he cannot learn to read. Is this true?"

"My 18-year-old has autism and Down syndrome. She reads at the second grade level. Are there tests that can be used to assess a child with severe intellectual disabilities?"

"What are the legal requirements for the transition assessment process?"

"My child's written work is full of spelling errors. I don't know if her problems are due to a learning disability or lack of teaching. Can I request that the school evaluate her?"

"My child was tested on two tests and earned different scores. Which test should we rely on?"

What is in This Book?

In *Wrightslaw: All About Tests and Assessments*, you will learn how to prepare for an assessment and what a comprehensive assessment should include.

You will learn how to request an evaluation by the school and how to provide parental consent. You will learn the steps to determine if a child is eligible for special education services.

You will find charts of tests and skills. The charts list tests to evaluate specific problems, the skills your child needs in these areas, and shows which tests measure these skills.

We introduce you to test terms because you need to be familiar with these terms. Our goal is to demystify tests and assessments and make them less intimidating.

As you read these questions and answers, you may feel like you are having a conversation with Pete, Pam, and Melissa. When you read a question that captures your interest, you wonder what advice we will give.

You will learn two important realities about tests and assessments. First, a test may not measure what it appears to measure. Second, a test may not measure your child's skills comprehensively.

You will learn that your child's test scores do not tell the whole story. Small differences between tests can result in large differences in scores.

How the Book is Organized

The questions and scenarios in *Wrightslaw: All About Tests and Assessment* are organized by topic into fifteen chapters. The book includes more than 200 questions and answers, including these:

- How are neuropsychological evaluations different from psycho-educational evaluations? Who does these assessments? (Chapter 1 – So Your Think Your Child Needs an Evaluation?)

- A school psychologist evaluated my child. The evaluation report did not include any recommendations. Shouldn't an evaluation include recommendations? (Chapter 2 – Evaluations by the School)

- What is a stanine? What is a standard deviation? Can I use age- and grade-equivalent scores to measure my child's progress? (Chapter 3 – Making Sense of Your Child's Test Scores)

- My daughter has autism and weak oral language skills. Can we get an accurate picture of her intelligence? (Chapter 4 – Intellectual Evaluations and IQ Testing)

- My son is in the first grade. He struggles to read. How can his scores on the Standardized Reading Inventory, Second Edition, be in the average range? (Chapter 6 – Reading Assessments)

- My child struggles with writing and spelling. What should an assessment of written language include? (Chapter 7 – Writing and Spelling Assessments)

- What role does working memory play in difficulties with math? (Chapter 8 – Mathematics and Math Assessments)

- My first grader's speech is difficult to understand. Is he too young to be tested? (Chapter 9 – Speech and Language Assessments)

- My son is bright but he has always struggled to learn in school. Should I have him evaluated for a learning disability? (Chapter 10 – Evaluations for Learning Disabilities and Attention-Deficit/ Hyperactivity Disorders (ADHD))

- An audiologist advised us that our daughter has a mild-to-moderate hearing loss. Should we be concerned? (Chapter 11 – Assessments of Hearing, Vision, and Motor Skills)

- My daughter has difficulty remembering and following directions. Her doctor says she needs to be tested for an auditory processing disorder. What do I need to know? (Chapter 12 – Auditory, Visual, Visual-Motor, and Sensory Processing Assessments)

- What does a behavior specialist look for when conducting a Functional Behavior Assessment (FBA)? (Chapter 13 – Adaptive Behavior and Functional Behavior Assessments)

- What tests should be included in my child's transition assessment? (Chapter 14 – Transition Assessments)

- Since few tests are available to measure the skills of ELLs, can an evaluator use tests that were standardized on English-speaking children? (Chapter 15 – Assessing English Language Learners (ELLs))

Wrightslaw: All About Tests and Assessment includes recommended resources, a glossary of assessment terms, a master table of tests

All About Tests and Assessments

- with test name, age range, type of test, author, publisher, publisher website, and a comprehensive index.

Who Should Read This Book?

If you are a parent, you need to be an effective advocate for your child. To be an effective advocate, you must become an expert on your child and how he learns.

You need to learn about psychological and academic tests, their strengths and weaknesses, and what different tests measure. Depending on your child's difficulties, you may need to learn about speech-language, physical and occupational therapy, processing, adaptive behavior, and/or functional behavior assessments.

You also need to learn how to use test scores to monitor your child's progress or regression.

If are a teacher or a related service provider, you may receive confusing information about your students' test results. You need to learn how to find accurate, reliable information about the tests and assessments used with your students.

If you teach special education, school psychology, school administration, or education law courses, your students need to know how to find answers to their questions about what the law requires of them.

If you are an attorney or advocate who represents children with disabilities, you need to have a copy of *Wrightslaw: All About Tests and Assessments* on your desk and in your briefcase.

How to Use This Book

At the end of each chapter are endnotes. The endnotes are the authority we relied upon in our answers. When you take this book to school meetings (and we hope you will), you will know the law, regulation, article, or publication that supports each answer.

Federal laws and regulations are the minimum standards that public schools must comply with. Compliance with the law is not optional.

Updates: New editions of tests are published often. The legal requirements for evaluations may change in the future. Updates will be published here: www.wrightslaw.com/bks/aat/updates.htm

What This Book is Not About

Wrightslaw: All About Tests and Assessments is a book of frequently asked questions, not an encyclopedia of every question a parent, teacher, or advocate may have. The book is not primarily about eligibility or how to measure your child's educational progress. We expect to publish books on those topics in the future.

Are You Ready?

It's time to learn about tests and assessments. Grab your pen or highlighter and turn this page.

So You Think Your Child Needs an Evaluation?

- When to Have Your Child Evaluated
- Finding a Good Evaluator
- Parent Questions and Concerns
- Evaluation Report and Parent Feedback Meeting
- Test References

When your child is not meeting his developmental milestones or is struggling academically, behaviorally, or socially, you need to find out why. Getting help for your child begins with a comprehensive assessment to identify problems. For example:

Your child is seeing a therapist for depression and anxiety. Her therapist needs more information about these problems so she can address them in therapy.

Your child's behavior changed at home and in the community. She is aggressive and bullies younger children. She has no friends in the neighborhood.

All About Tests and Assessments

As a baby, your child seemed to develop normally. By age two, his vocabulary was over 100 words. After his second birthday, he stopped talking and no longer makes eye contact. You have a sinking feeling. Does your child have autism?

Your spouse is in the military and was deployed recently. Your child is usually a happy-go-lucky kid. Since his dad left, he is anxious and has frequent nightmares.

Although parents are usually the first to know that their child is struggling, they may not know what the problem is or what to do about it. This chapter will provide information about assessments and tests that are designed to answer your questions.

When to Have Your Child Evaluated

If your child is having academic, social, or behavioral problems, you may consider getting an evaluation. Or your child's school may ask for consent to evaluate your child. A comprehensive evaluation will identify your child's strengths, deficits, and needs. An evaluation will help you develop a plan to help your child and a roadmap for the future.

What happens in an assessment?

In an assessment, an evaluator gathers information about your child's knowledge and skills. A comprehensive assessment should include:

- Background and family history

- Formal and informal testing

- Observations in the classroom and other settings, if appropriate

- Interviews with parents, teachers, and the child

- Additional testing, depending on the presenting problem and test findings

Depending on your child's age and difficulties, an evaluator will assess your child in several areas that may include:

- Language skills

- Academic skills in reading, writing, and math

- Intelligence or cognitive ability

- Attention, memory, and processing speed

- Neurological functioning

- Fine and gross motor skills

- Social and emotional functioning

If your child has language problems, these difficulties are likely to affect reading, writing, math, class participation, and interaction with peers.

Intelligence tests measure your child's ability to learn, memory, phonological processing, processing speed, and other skills. Academic achievement tests measure reading, writing, and math skills.

The evaluation should include observations of your child's behavior during testing and may include observations of his behavior in the classroom or at home. Classroom work samples are another source of information.[1]

The evaluator will obtain information about your child's background and his educational and medical history from parents, teachers, and your child.

The assessment should answer your questions and include strategies and recommendations about what your child needs. The evaluator may identify professionals who can help your child.

Who can conduct an evaluation?

The evaluation will be conducted by an examiner who has a master's degree or doctoral degree in education or psychology. One examiner or several specialists who have expertise in specific areas may be involved. Qualifications of evaluators vary between the public and private sectors and from state to state.

When is a neuropsychological evaluation useful?

A neuropsychological evaluation is useful if your child's intellectual/cognitive functioning, behavior, or learning may be impaired. For example, you may be referred for a neuropsychological assessment if your child has:

- Traumatic brain injury (TBI)

- Developmental disabilities

- Learning disabilities and/or Attention-Deficit/Hyperactivity Disorder (ADHD)

- An autism spectrum disorder

- Psychiatric disorders

What should be included in a neuropsychological evaluation?

A neuropsychologist may assess:

- Intelligence

- Language

- Attention and memory

- Perceptual abilities

- Emotion and personality factors

- Behavior regulation

- Organization, judgment, planning, efficiency at producing work

Some neuropsychological evaluations include academic skills.

A neuropsychological evaluation should be conducted by a licensed psychologist or licensed neuropsychologist who has training and expertise in neuropsychology.

How are neuropsychological evaluations different from psycho-educational evaluations?

Neuropsychological evaluations are usually broader in scope than psycho-educational evaluations.

A neuropsychologist may focus more on processes related to learning and executive functioning —memory, attention, organization, and the ability to regulate behavior.

All About Tests and Assessments

What are the differences between tests, evaluations, and assessments?

A test refers to a single test that is used to collect data. An assessment includes formal and informal tests, observations, and interviews. During an assessment, the examiner collects data, integrates findings, interprets results, and makes recommendations. The terms *assessment* and *evaluation* are often used interchangeably.

How is an evaluation by an examiner in the private sector different from an evaluation by the school?

A privately obtained evaluation should answer your questions and include specific recommendations about what your child needs. The evaluation should include a diagnosis and recommendations. It may include referrals to other service providers like psychotherapists, speech-language therapists, and academic tutors.

Your child's school evaluates children to determine if they are eligible for special education services and accommodations. You will learn about school evaluations in Chapter 2.

Finding a Good Evaluator

An evaluation is only as good as the evaluator. Finding a qualified evaluator is similar to finding a medical specialist. Your goal is to find a professional who is knowledgeable about child development and skilled at interpreting test results.

Good recommendations come from satisfied clients. Do you know parents, friends, or relatives whose child has been evaluated? What were their experiences?

Ask professionals who refer children for evaluations—doctors and mental health experts—for their recommendations. You can also contact parent support groups, child advocates, and special education schools.

What education and training do evaluators have?

The answer to this question depends on the type of evaluation. If your child needs a psycho-educational evaluation, the examiner should have a master's or doctoral degree in education, clinical psychology, or school psychology. If your child needs a neuropsychological evaluation, the evaluator will have a doctoral degree in psychology and training in neuropsychology.

Speech-language pathologists who assess speech and language problems have master's degrees. Audiologists should have a master's or doctoral degree in audiology. Audiologists who test a child's hearing should have pediatric educational experience. Behavior specialists should be certified in Behavioral Analysis.

Evaluators should have the credentials required by the laws of your state. They should be trained according to the requirements of test publishers.

Chapter 1. So You Think Your Child Needs an Evaluation?

Professionals should be willing to answer questions about their education, training, and experience. You should check references and review credentials.

How will the evaluator know what tests to use?

When the reasons for the referral are clear, the evaluator can select tests to address your areas of concern. You can help by providing specific information about your concerns.

For example, if your child is anxious, has nightmares, and does not want to attend school, describe these problems. Give examples. When did the problems begin? Are they getting worse? Do you have ideas about why?

Assume that your child has difficulty writing stories and papers. His handwriting is illegible and he misspells words. When you meet with the evaluator, describe your child's specific writing problems in detail. Provide samples of his work.

Perhaps your child struggles to complete school assignments. He cannot remember what he reads. You may say, "It takes hours for him to finish a short reading assignment," or "When he finishes a reading assignment, he does not remember what he read. He can't answer questions about it."

Does your child receive private tutoring? Do you provide help with homework? The evaluator needs to know about this extra help.

All this information will help the evaluator select the right tests for your child. This will ensure that the evaluation produces an accurate picture of your child and factors that are affecting him.

When I scheduled the appointment for my child's assessment, the evaluator said she wants to meet with me ahead of time. What should I do to prepare?

Good question! The evaluator needs to know your child's background and history. When you meet with the evaluator, come prepared to answer questions about your child's:

- Pregnancy and birth

- Developmental milestones

- Health, illnesses, and medications

- Behavior, social and emotional functioning

- Family history of learning and/or psychological problems

The evaluator will review your child's health history. Be sure to share any earlier assessments. Bring copies of evaluations, report cards, and educational interventions. Were these interventions effective?

Be prepared to describe your child's relationships with family members, neighbors, peers, and even pets. Has his attitude or behavior changed? How? When? What are his academic problems and homework issues?

All About Tests and Assessments

Don't focus on the negative! Include information about your child's strengths and interests. Be sure to include what gets his attention and what makes him happy.

Will the evaluator get information about my child from other sources?

Yes, evaluators gather information from many sources. You need to share medical, psychological, and educational information with your evaluator. If your child is in therapy or sees a specialist, the evaluator may ask for your consent to consult with those professionals.

The evaluator may ask you and your child's teachers to complete questionnaires and behavior rating forms.

Parent Questions and Concerns

What should I tell my child about why he is being tested?

Be low-key about the evaluation. You don't want to send a message that your child did something wrong. Connect the evaluation to a problem he has: "Your trouble reading," "Problems you have understanding directions," or "You get upset easily."

Explain that there are different ways to learn. The evaluator wants to find out what his teachers have taught him and how his teachers can make learning easier.

My child has a disability. Will this make evaluating her more difficult?

Not really. Most evaluators are experienced in evaluating children with disabilities.

Look for an evaluator who is knowledgeable about your child's disability. Contact your state or regional disability organizations and ask for a list of recommended evaluators in your state.

Your state Parent Training and Information Center is a good source of information about appropriate evaluators.

When you prepare your child for the evaluation, this will minimize her anxiety and encourage cooperation.

What do you say when your child asks, "Why do I have to take these tests?"

"These tests are not like the tests you take at school. These tests will tell us how you learn. When you get frustrated with your _____ (homework/ handwriting/ math problems/ boredom/ attention/ behavior), your mind is telling you, 'I would learn more if I could do it this way.' We need to find out how we can make school better for you.

"The evaluation will include questions, puzzles, drawings, and stories. Some parts will be easy, others will be harder, and some will be fun."

My child takes medication for ADHD. Should she be tested on medication or off medication?

As a rule, if your child is diagnosed with ADHD and takes stimulant medication, she should take the medication as it is prescribed. Check with the examiner before the evaluation so you can coordinate the evaluation with the dosage time. See Chapter 10 for more about about Evaluations for Learning Disabilities and Attention-Deficit/ Hyperactivity Disorders (ADHD)..

What else can I do to prepare my child for the evaluation?

Be sure your child has a good night's sleep and a good breakfast before the evaluation.

Tell your child what to expect. When he has information about the place, time, and the evaluator, he will be less anxious. For example, make sure your child knows that he will be meeting alone with the evaluator. Tell him about how much time the testing will take. Let him know where you will be during the evaluation in case he needs you.

Your child needs to know that you expect him to do his best.

Evaluation Report and Parent Feedback Meeting

Will I receive a report from the evaluator?

Yes, the evaluator will prepare a written report for you. Review this report carefully. Take notes. Highlight areas that are not clear to you. If you see mistakes in your child's background history, advise the evaluator.

After the evaluation, you and the evaluator will meet for a parent feedback meeting. She will describe her findings and

recommendations. Ask the evaluator to describe your child's problems and learning style in language you understand.

Ask the evaluator for permission to record the feedback meeting so you can review it later. Do not be afraid to ask questions!

What should an evaluation report include?

The evaluation report should include:

- Identifying and referral information

- Presenting problems, symptoms, and parental concerns

- Early development, family history, school problems

- Speech and language development

- Social development

- Interviews with the parent and child

- Behavioral observations of the child

- Tests administered and test results

- Recommendations [2]

I am glad we've decided to get the facts about my child's problems. So why am I so nervous about this evaluation?

When you are a parent, it is natural to question yourself when you decide to have your child evaluated. You have concerns about her emotional well-being. Most parents wonder . . .

All About Tests and Assessments

- Is my child normal? Is something wrong with her?

- What does she need?

- What is her diagnosis? What does the diagnosis mean?

- Will she be traumatized by an evaluation with a stranger?

- Am I to blame? Did I do something to cause her problems?

If you are like many parents, you feel nagging doubts followed by hopes that your worries are silly and unfounded. You may cling to advice that "Everything is ok. This is just a phase that she will outgrow." These thoughts can prevent you from taking action.

If you take a "wait and see" approach, your child will not get the help she needs. If you think your child has a problem, have her evaluated. Don't delay.

So many tests are used to assess children. Is there one test that gives good baseline information in all areas of need?

Unfortunately, no test provides good baseline information in all areas.

Intelligence (IQ) tests, educational achievement tests, behavior assessments, and speech and language assessments measure different areas and skills. When selecting appropriate tests, the evaluator will keep your child's profile in mind.

The next chapters in this book will describe different types of tests that may be used in your child's assessment.

Test References

Is there a book or resource that lists all the tests used in evaluations?

Sorry, no book or website lists all tests. But there are resources that will answer most of your questions.

Start with a test reference that is available on-line or through your local library. These references provide comprehensive, useful information and answer questions like these:

- What tests are available for a specific issue (e.g., language delay)?

- Who publishes the test?

- What are the strengths and weaknesses of the test?

- How can I get more information on a particular test?

Tests in Print (TIP), the *Mental Measurements Yearbook* (MMY), *Tests*, and *Test Critiques* are popular references. These references are available in the reference section of most college, university, and larger public libraries.

Tests in Print (TIP) is a bibliographic encyclopedia of information on published tests of psychology and achievement. http://buros.org/tests-print

In the *Mental Measurements Yearbook* (MMY), tests are listed by name or title. Many entries include reviews of the test and test materials by psychologists. http://buros.org/mental-measurements-yearbook

The Test Locator is a gateway to information about tests. Sponsors include Ericae.net, Buros Institute of Mental Measurements, and ETS TestLink. http://ericae.net/testcol.htm

Test Reviews Online is a web-based service. For a fee, individuals can examine information on over 2,000 tests (test purpose, population, publication date, administration, and test critiques). http://buros.unl.edu/buros/jsp/search.jsp

The *Southwest Educational Development Laboratory* (SEDL) website has a database of reading assessments for children from pre-kindergarten through Grade 3. www.sedl.org/reading/rad/

The *Willis Dumont* website by John O. Willis and Ron Dumont provides commentary and reviews of assessments, often with a dose of humor that may make you laugh. http://alpha.fdu.edu/psychology/extended_links.htm

In Summation

In this chapter, you got an overview of evaluations, assessments, and tests. You learned how to find an evaluator and steps to take in preparing your child for an evaluation. You learned where to find information about the tests used by evaluators.

This information is your starting point. Keep going. Don't let your worries or fears prevent you from doing the right thing for your child. When you arm yourself with knowledge, your anxiety will drop and your child will get the help he needs.

Knowledge is power . . . and you are about to get a lot more powerful.

Endnotes

1. Sattler, J. (2008). *Assessment of children: cognitive foundations* (5th ed.). San Diego, CA: Author

2. Farrall, M.L. (2012). *Reading assessment; Linking language, literacy, and cognition.* Hoboken, NJ: John Wiley & Sons, Inc., p. 319

2 Evaluations by the School

- The Child Find Mandate

- Evaluations for Special Education

- Getting to Know School Evaluators

- Requesting an Evaluation and Providing Consent

- Information and Observations

- Independent Educational Evaluations (IEEs)

- Determining Eligibility

If your child is struggling, the school may ask to do an evaluation on your child. If you are concerned about your child's progress, you may ask the school to evaluate your child. For example:

Your child is fidgety and distractible. When you ask her doctor if she may have ADHD, the doctor suggests that you ask the school to evaluate your child.

Your third grader struggles to read and says he hates school. His grades have dropped. He may be retained. Does he have a learning disability?

Your seventh grader skips school and gets into fights with other kids. He has been suspended several times.

All About Tests and Assessments

In this chapter, you will learn about the school district's responsibilities to evaluate your child. You will learn about the Child Find Mandate, special education evaluations, school evaluators, and eligibility for special education and related services.

Schools evaluate to...

- Identify children who are experiencing delays or learning problems

- Determine if a child has a disability and is eligible for special education and related services

- Identify a child's needs for special education and related services

- Gather functional, developmental, and academic information about a child

- Gather data about a child's present levels of academic achievement, functional performance, and educational needs that will be used to develop an appropriate Individualized Education Program (IEP)

- Provide information to help teachers and related service personnel provide appropriate instruction, services and accommodations

- Monitor a child's progress in a special education program

As a parent, you need to know about assessments and tests, their strengths and weaknesses, and what tests actually measure. You also need to learn how to use test scores to monitor your child's progress or regression.

The Child Find Mandate

The Individuals with Disabilities Education Act (IDEA) is the federal special education law. The law includes a Child Find Mandate that requires states to identify, locate, and evaluate all children, from birth through age 21, who may have a disability and need special education services.[1]

The Child Find Mandate applies to all children, including:

- Children who attend private schools and public schools

- Highly mobile children

- Migrant children

- Homeless children

- Children who are wards of the state

The requirements to identify and evaluate apply to all children who may have a disability, including children who receive passing grades and are "advancing from grade to grade." [2]

Evaluations for Special Education

If the school thinks your child may have a disability, they will request your written consent before evaluating your child. You also have the right to ask the school to evaluate your child. This evaluation is at no cost to your family.

The evaluation must assess all areas related to your child's suspected disability, including:

- Health

- Vision and hearing

- Social and emotional status

- General intelligence

- Academic performance

- Communication abilities

- Motor abilities

Tests and assessments must be:

- Valid and reliable

- Administered by trained, knowledgeable examiners according to the test publisher's instructions

- Given in your child's native language or primary mode of communication

When evaluating your child, the school may not:

- Use tests or assessments that are racially or culturally discriminatory

- Use any single test or assessment to determine if your child has a disability [3]

After the evaluation, the school will provide you with a copy of the evaluation report at no charge to you.

Getting to Know School Evaluators

Who from the school will evaluate my child?

Earlier in this chapter, you learned that the school is required to assess all areas related to your child's suspected disability. Depending on your child's needs, she may be evaluated by:

- Speech and language pathologists

- Physical therapists, occupational therapists

- School psychologists

- Special education teachers, reading specialists

- Audiologists, experts in vision and hearing

- Other professionals

What education and training do school psychologists have?

The National Association of School Psychologists establishes ethical and training standards for school psychologists. At a minimum, a school psychologist must have a master's degree in school psychology. School psychologists must be certified and/or licensed by the state in which they work. [4]

When I reviewed the results of the Woodcock-Johnson III on my child, the evaluator was my child's teacher. Is a teacher qualified as an evaluator?

Maybe. The publishers of the *Woodcock-Johnson® III Normative Update Tests of Achievement (WJ III ACH)* **recommend** (but do not require) that examiners have graduate-level training in educational assessment and a background in diagnostic decision-making.

All About Tests and Assessments

The publishers of the *Woodcock-Johnson® III Normative Update (NU) Tests of Cognitive Abilities (WJ III COG)* **require** examiners to have graduate-level training in assessing cognitive ability and a background in diagnostic decision-making.[5]

Requesting an Evaluation and Providing Consent

How can I request an evaluation for special education?

If you think your child may have a disability and need special education services, write a letter to request an evaluation. Include your observations, concerns, questions, and a statement that you give your informed consent for the evaluation.

See the sample letter to request an evaluation for special education services in Table 2-1. You can revise this letter to reflect your child's circumstances.

When I ask the school to evaluate my child, what information should I provide?

You are more likely to get a useful evaluation if you provide the team with a written description of your concerns and questions before the evaluation. Be sure to include background information about your child and describe your concerns. Your information will help the team select appropriate tests to measure your child's skills and deficits.

Can the school decide what areas they will test?

Yes. The school team determines the areas they will test, but they are required to assess your child in *all areas* related to the suspected disability. The school evaluation must be comprehensive and must include "a variety of assessment tools and strategies to gather relevant functional, developmental, and academic information about the child, including information provided by the parent."[6]

Must I give written consent before the school can evaluate my child?

Yes. The school cannot evaluate your child until after you give your *informed written consent*. Informed written consent means that:

- You were informed about the school's plans to evaluate in your native language

- You understand and "agree in writing" that the school may evaluate your child

You may revoke your consent at any time.[7]

I wrote a letter to request an evaluation for special education and included my informed consent statement. The school says I have to sign their legal consent form.

The law does not require parents to sign a legal consent form developed by a school district. But do not let a battle over school policies slow down or stop your child's evaluation. Sign and return the school's "legal consent" form today.

Table 2-1. Sample Letter to Request an Evaluation for Special Education

Jane Smith
500 Oak Lane
Centerville, IL 60010
899-555-1234
Date

George Williams, Principal
Grove Elementary School
1000 Main Street
Middleburg, IL 60010

Reference: Ryan Smith
             DOB: 01/02/2004
             School: Grove Elementary School

Dear Mr. Williams:

I am writing to ask that the school evaluate Ryan Smith for special education services. Ryan is 10 years old, in the fourth grade, and has not learned how to read.

Ryan has struggled in school since kindergarten. He was retained in first grade. His reading and spelling skills are poor. He cannot read the labels on cans at the grocery store. His handwriting is illegible.

His teachers have given him extra help. I obtained private tutoring for him twice a week. Despite this extra help, his reading and spelling skills have not improved. He is very anxious and depressed. He says he is "stupid" and wants to quit school.

I understand that the school needs my written consent before evaluating Ryan. Please consider this letter my consent to evaluate. I understand that a decision about Ryan's eligibility for special education will be made within 60 days. [Note: Check your state special education regulations for the timeline in your state.]

I want to speak with the psychologist before the evaluation. If you have questions, please call me at work (555-9876) or at home (555-1234) after 6:00 pm.

Sincerely,

Jane Smith

All About Tests and Assessments

What happens if I don't give my consent for the school to evaluate my child?

The school is required to evaluate your child and provide the special education services he needs. If you do not give your consent, the school district may request a due process hearing against you.

How long does the school have to evaluate and determine if my child is eligible for special education services?

After receiving your informed written consent, the school must evaluate your child and determine if she is eligible for special education within *60 calendar days* unless your state has a different timeline.[8]

The federal special education law allows states to adopt longer and shorter timelines. Be sure to check your state's special education regulations to find the timeline in your state.

Information and Observations

Tests alone will not provide a comprehensive picture of your child's strengths, weaknesses, and educational needs. The examiner should gather information from other sources. The examiner is likely to:

- Observe your child in the classroom and other settings to see how she functions in different environments

- Interview you, your child, and others who know your child

Observations in the classroom and in other settings provide valuable information about your child's ability to learn.

Is the school required to observe my child in the classroom?

If the school is evaluating your child for a specific learning disability, the team is required to do a classroom observation.[9] You will learn more about evaluations for Learning Disabilities in Chapter 10.

If the school is evaluating your child for a different disability — autism, Attention-Deficit/ Hyperactivity Disorder (ADHD), or a hearing impairment — the law allows but does not **require** a classroom observation.

Request an observation in the classroom and in other settings where there are concerns. It is also helpful to observe in a classroom where your child does well. What is it about that setting that helps your child to learn?

What happens during a classroom observation?

An educator will observe your child's behavior and how the teacher and other students interact with your child. The school team needs to answer these questions:

- Who will observe?

- When and where will the observation occur?

- How will the observation be recorded?

Multiple observations will provide a more reliable sample of your child's behavior.

Observations can be made in different situations or locations, and at different times.

The school is evaluating my child for a learning disability. A psychologist observed him during Physical Education (PE). Shouldn't the psychologist observe him in the classroom?

Yes. The observation needs to focus on your child's performance in the regular education classroom. An observation of your child in PE will not provide useful information about your child's reading difficulties or their impact on his academic performance.

Request an observation—in writing. Describe your concerns that the psychologist's observation of your son in PE did not provide useful information about his learning in the classroom.

My child's evaluation included computer-generated reports. Are these reports as accurate as reports written by an examiner?

No. A computer-generated report cannot consider your child's history, previous test results, and instruction.

Some tests provide an option to create computer-generated reports that describe your child's strengths and weaknesses. These reports can be customized to a limited degree but do not provide the benefit of an expert's eye.

My child's psychological evaluation report did not include recommendations. Shouldn't an evaluation report by a school psychologist include recommendations?

Yes, the school psychologist's report should include recommendations, along with strategies and interventions that may help your child. If the psychologist thinks your child's educational program needs to be modified, he should discuss these recommendations with you and your child's team.[10]

Independent Educational Evaluations (IEEs)

The school evaluated my child. I don't agree with their findings or their recommendations. What can I do?

If you disagree with the school district's evaluation and/or recommendations, you have the right to request an Independent Educational Evaluation (IEE) at the school district's expense. The IEE must be conducted by a qualified examiner who is not employed by the school district. At a minimum, the IEE should determine if your child has or continues to have a disability, and your child's educational needs.[11]

If you request an IEE at the school district's expense, the district must ensure that your child receives the IEE or request a due process hearing to prove that its original evaluation is appropriate.

All About Tests and Assessments

School districts often attempt to restrict the parent's choice of evaluators to a list of approved evaluators selected by the school. The Office of Special Education Programs issued a policy letter clarifying that parents have the right to choose their own independent evaluator.[12]

Getting an IEE, especially if you want to select the evaluator, can be a touchy issue. You need to proceed carefully. It may be a good idea to consult with an attorney who has expertise in special education matters before requesting an IEE.

Learn more about IEEs at www.wrightslaw.com/info/test.index.htm and in *Wrightslaw: Special Education Law, 2nd ed.* www.wrightslaw.com/bks/selaw2/selaw2.htm

We obtained a comprehensive evaluation of our child by a psychologist in the private sector. We provided the evaluation to our child's team. The team said they considered the evaluation and decided not to use any information or recommendations from it. Can they do that?

The law does not require the team to accept the findings or implement recommendations from a specialist in the private sector.[13] The law does require the school to respond to your concerns about your child's educational program.

The law also requires the IEP team to *consider* the results of any evaluation you obtain.[14]

What does "consider" mean?

The dictionary defines "consider" as "to think about carefully in order to arrive at a judgment or decision, especially with regard to taking some action."[15]

The federal special education regulations impose an "affirmative obligation" on the school team to consider the results of any evaluation.[16] In one case, a federal court ruled that the school's failure to consider private evaluations submitted by the parents was a serious violation of the law that denied the child's right to a free, appropriate public education.[17]

It is easier to "consider" and reject an evaluation if the evaluator is not present to describe her findings and recommendations. If you get an evaluation from a specialist in the private sector, ask her to attend the meeting to discuss her findings.

When the evaluator is available to describe the child's needs, program, and recommendations, it is more likely that the IEP team will accept and use the evaluation results.

Determining Eligibility

After the school completes the evaluation, a team that includes school professionals and the child's parent will meet to review the evaluation results.

The team will decide if your child is a "child with a disability" and is eligible for special

education and related services. To be eligible, your child must meet **two criteria**.

- She must have a disability that adversely affects her educational performance.
- She must **need** special education and related services.[18]

Can I request a copy of the school's evaluation report before an eligibility meeting?

Yes, you should request a copy of the report before the meeting. Make your request in writing. When you have the evaluation report ahead of time, this will help you prepare for the meeting.

Some states require schools to provide evaluation reports before eligibility meetings. Check your state special education regulations to find out what is required in your state.

After the eligibility meeting, you are entitled to a copy of the evaluation report and documentation of eligibility at no cost.[19]

My child was found eligible for special education. What happens next?

After your child is found eligible for services, the team will use information from the evaluation to develop the Individualized Education Program (IEP).[20] If your child is an infant from birth to three years, information from the evaluation will be incorporated into her Individualized Family Service Plan (IFSP).

In Summation

In this chapter, you learned about the Child Find Mandate that requires states to locate, identify, and evaluate all children, from birth to age 21, who may have a disability. These evaluations must be comprehensive and at no cost to the families.

You learned how to request an evaluation in writing and how to provide informed parental consent. You learned about the steps to determine if a child is eligible for special education services.

In the next chapter, you will learn about test scores - how to interpret test scores, and how use test scores to monitor your child's progress in a special education program.

Endnotes

1. 20 U.S.C. §1414(b)(2), 34 C.F.R. §300.304

2. 20 U.S.C. §1412(a)(3), 34 C.F.R §300.111

3. 20 U.S.C. §1414(b)(3), 34 C.F.R. §300.304

4. State School Psychology Credentialing Requirements. Retrieved from www.nasponline.org/certification/state_info_list.aspx

5. *Woodcock-Johnson® III Normative Update (NU) Tests of Cognitive Abilities.* (n.d.). Retrieved from

   www.riverpub.com/products/wjIIICognitive/details.html

6. 20 U.S.C. §1414(b)(2), 34 C.F.R. §300.304

7. 20 U.S.C. §1414 (a)(1)(D), 34 C.F.R. §300.300

8. 20 U.S.C. §1414(a)(1)(C), 34 C.F.R. §300.301

9. 34 C.F.R. §300.310

10. National Association of School Psychologists. (2010) *Principles for Professional Ethics, Standard II.* Retrieved from www.nasponline.org/standards/2010standards/1_%20Ethical%20Principles.pdf

11. 20 U.S.C. §1415(b)(1)

12. OSEP Letter to Parker (2004) at www.wrightslaw.com/info/test.eval.choice.osep.htm

13. 34 C.F.R. §300.502(c)(1)

14. 34 C.F.R. §300.502(c); Commentary in 71 FR at 46690

15. Merriam-Webster Dictionary Online. www.merriam-webster.com/dictionary/consider

16. www.wrightslaw.com/idea/comment/46688-46713.reg.501-520.procedures.pdf p.46690

17. *DiBuo v. Bd. Of Educ. of Worcester County,* slip no. S-01-1311 (Nov. 14, 2001), www.wrightslaw.com/info/test.iee.steedman.htm

18. 20 U.S.C. §1401(3)

19. 20 U.S.C. §1414(b)(4), 34 C.F.R. §300.306(a)(2)

20. 20 U.S.C. §1414(c)(1)

Making Sense of Your Child's Test Scores

- Understanding Your Child's Test Scores

- Norm-Referenced Tests and Criterion-Referenced Tests

- The Bell Curve

- Test Scores

- Subtest Scores, Composite Scores, and Index Scores

- Measuring Educational Progress

To be an effective advocate, you need to understand the child's scores on tests and assessments. Test scores provide information about the child's abilities, academic achievement, and functional performance.

When you understand test scores, you will be able to answer these questions:

- What are the child's strengths and weaknesses?

- What does the child need in his educational program?

- How can I monitor the child's progress or lack of progress?

All About Tests and Assessments

If your child has an Individualized Education Program (IEP), the school team will use scores from tests and assessments to determine the present levels of academic achievement and functional performance. The scores will be used to develop goals in the IEP.

In this chapter, you will learn about standardized norm-referenced tests and criterion-referenced tests. You will also learn about academic and diagnostic assessments, the bell curve, standard scores, T scores, stanines, subtest scores, standard deviations, and percentile ranks.

You will learn why you should never rely on one test or one test score when making decisions about your child's educational programming and remediation of specific skill deficits. When you understand what test scores mean, you will be able to use test results to monitor your child's progress.

Although test scores are important, they should not be your only source of information. First, tests may not measure what they appear to measure. Second, all tests do not measure a child's skills comprehensively. Third, even the best tests are not perfectly reliable.

Understanding Your Child's Test Scores

Assume you attend an IEP meeting for your child with a learning disability. Your child's teachers say, "We are so excited. Your child earned a score of 85 on the reading test!"

As you will learn in this chapter, if your child earns a standard score of 85 (SS = 85) on a test, his percentile rank is 16 (PR = 16). Eighty-four percent of his peers earned higher scores on the test. Your child was in the 16th percentile rank. Are you excited to learn that your child earned a percentile rank of 16 in reading?

What skills did the reading test measure? Did the child's scores improve, stay the same, or drop?

Norm-Referenced Tests and Criterion-Referenced Tests

Standardized, norm-referenced tests are used to assess many areas, including intelligence and academic skills. These tests are also used to measure specific skills required for reading, written language, and math. To learn about academic achievement tests, see Chapters 5 through 8.

A standardized test is given the same way to all children. Evaluators follow rules for test administration. Evaluators are not permitted to alter materials or reword questions.

Standardized, norm-referenced tests provide valuable information about your child's levels of functioning in the areas tested. Norm-referenced tests also provide a way to evaluate changes in performance, including the impact of educational remediation.

What are norm-referenced tests?

Norm-referenced tests are standardized tests that compare one child's performance with the performance of other children in the same age or grade. Norm-referenced tests use scoring systems that are designed to capture a child's skills with respect to the peer group.

What are criterion-referenced tests?

Criterion-referenced tests are used to measure knowledge or skills. The child's score is based on mastery of the material and is usually expressed as a percentage.

Teachers use criterion-referenced tests to determine if students have mastered material. Classroom spelling and math tests are criterion-referenced tests. A child who spells 8 of 10 words correctly on a spelling test will earn a score of 80%.

What are the differences between norm-referenced and criterion-referenced tests?

Norm-referenced tests allow you to compare one child's performance to a representative sample of his peers. You can compare your child's score to scores of other children who are the same age or in the same grade.

Criterion-referenced tests are used to assess academic knowledge and skills in greater depth. For example, a criterion-referenced test can show if your child has mastered specific math facts or phonics skills.

Before you can fully understand your child's test scores, you need to understand a few basic concepts: the bell curve, mean, and standard deviation. If you take the time to learn about test scores, you will have the knowledge to change your child's life.

The Bell Curve

You need to know how your child is performing on tests, when compared to other children at the same age or grade level. The bell curve will provide this information and allow you to create graphs to show progress or lack of progress.

The bell curve is a graph showing the percentage of children who earn scores from low to high. When all scores are plotted on the graph, it forms a bell shape. Most children are in the "average" range so the curve is the highest in the middle. There are fewer high and low scores.

Before you can use the bell curve, you need to know the Mean and Standard Deviation of a test. The Mean and the Standard Deviation are the keys to interpreting test scoring systems.

What is the Mean?

On the bell curve, the Mean is in the middle, at the 50th percentile. The average or Mean score on most tests is 100 (Mean = 100). Tests are made up of subtests. The Mean is usually 10 on subtests (Mean = 10).

What are Standard Deviations?

The bell curve is measured in units called Standard Deviations (SD). Standard Deviations describe how far test scores spread out or deviate from the Mean. The center of the bell curve (the Mean) is at 0 (zero) Standard Deviations. A score that is zero Standard Deviations from the Mean is always at the 50th percentile (PR = 50).

27

All About Tests and Assessments

On the bell curve, the area between one Standard Deviation to the right (+1 SD) and 1 Standard Deviation to the left (-1 SD) of the Mean represents 68% (about two-thirds) of the population. If we increase the range to two Standard Deviations above (+2 SD) to two Standard Deviations below (-2 SD) the Mean, about 96% of the population is represented.

A score that is two Standard Deviations above the Mean is at or close to the 98th percentile (PR = 98). A score that is two Standard Deviations below the Mean is at or close to the 2nd percentile (PR =2).

Assume for a moment your child earned a score that is one Standard Deviation below the Mean (-1 SD). Do you know how your child performed when compared to his peers?

Figure 3-1. Bell Curve with Mean, Standard Deviations, Subtest Scores, Percentile Ranks

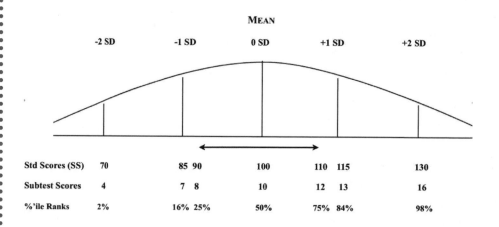

	-2 SD	-1 SD	0 SD	+1 SD	+2 SD
Std Scores (SS)	70	85 90	100	110 115	130
Subtest Scores	4	7 8	10	12 13	16
%'ile Ranks	2%	16% 25%	50%	75% 84%	98%

Figure 3-1 is a diagram of the bell curve with Standard Deviations, the percentage within each Standard Deviation, and percentile ranks. A score that is one Standard Deviation above the Mean is at or close to the 84th percentile rank (PR = 84). A score that is one Standard Deviation below the Mean is at or close to the 16th percentile (PR = 16). On some tests, the percentile ranks are close to, but not exactly at the expected value.

Now assume your child earned a score that is one Standard Deviation above the Mean (+ 1 SD). How did your child perform when compared to his peers?

For answers to these questions, see the Conversion Table in Figure 3-3.

On most psychological and educational tests, the mean is 100 and the Standard Deviation is 15 points. Evaluators usually provide the Mean and Standard Deviation in their evaluation report. When you know the Mean and Standard Deviation of a test, you can determine how your child is performing when compared to other children who are at his age or grade level.

Test Scores

What are raw scores?

The raw score describes the number of correct answers on a test or subtest, or the number of tasks performed correctly. The raw score can also measure the frequency of a behavior. Raw scores are converted into standard scores, percentile ranks, grade-equivalent, and age-equivalent scores.

What are standard scores?

Standard scores are raw scores that have been converted to have a Mean and Standard Deviation.

Most commonly used scoring systems have a Mean of 100 and a Standard Deviation of ±15. Scores between 85 and 115 capture the middle two-thirds of the children tested.

If your child earned a standard score (SS) of 100, this score is zero deviations from the Mean because it is at the Mean. If your child scores one Standard Deviation above the Mean (+1 SD), the standard score is 115 (100 + 15). If your child scored one Standard Deviation below the Mean (-1 SD), the standard score is 85 (100 − 15 = 85).

What are scaled scores?

Scaled scores are a standard score that has a Mean of 10 and a Standard Deviation of ± 3. Scores between 7 and 13 include the middle two-thirds of children tested. Most subtest scores are reported as scaled scores.

Figure 3-2. Bell Curve with Standard Deviations, Percentile Ranks, Standard Scores, and Subtest (Scale) Scores

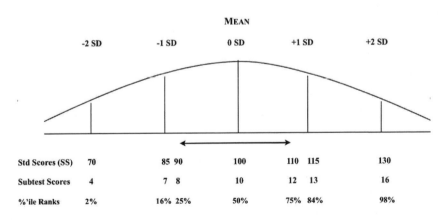

All About Tests and Assessments

If your child scores one Standard Deviation above the Mean (+1 SD), his standard score is 13 (10 + 3). If your child scores one Standard Deviation below the Mean (-1 SD), his standard score is 7 (10 − 3).

What are T Scores?

T scores are a type of standard score that has a Mean of 50 and a Standard Deviation of ± 10. If your child scores one Standard Deviation above the Mean (+ 1 SD), her T score is 60. If your child scores one Standard Deviation below the Mean (-1 SD), her T score is 40.

What are stanines?

Stanines are standard scores that have a Mean of 5 and a Standard Deviation of about ±2. If your child scores one Standard Deviation above the Mean (+ 1 SD), her stanine score is 7 (5 + 2). If her score is one Standard Deviation below the Mean (-1 SD), her stanine score is 3 (5 − 2).

What are percentile ranks?

Percentile ranks describe your child's rank or position when compared to other children who are the same age or in the same grade. Percentile ranks are not equal units. Percentile ranks cluster around the mean, and they stretch out at the low and high ends of the bell curve.

If your child earns a standard score of 100, your child's percentile rank is 50. This means that your child performed as well as or better than 50 percent of children who are his age or in his grade. If your child earns a percentile rank of 75 on a standardized test, your child scored as well or better than 75 percent of his peers. Percentile ranks are not the same as percent of correct answers on a test.

I need to know if my child is making progress. Can I convert standard scores into percentile ranks?

Yes. You can use Figure 3-3 to convert standard scores and scaled scores into percentile ranks, and percentile ranks into standard scores and scaled scores.

What are age- and grade-equivalent scores?

Age- and grade-equivalent scores are quick, easy ways to estimate your child's skill levels. Age-equivalent scores are reported as years and months (AE: 7-6 or 7:6). Grade-equivalent scores are reported as grades and months (GE: 7.6). Note: On most tests, a "month" equals one-tenth of a school year or 18 school days.

Age- and grade-equivalent scores are not equal units. Age- and grade-equivalent scores need to be explicit. An age-equivalent (AE) score of 7-6 means 7 years, 6 months.

A grade- equivalent (GE) score of 7.6 means 7th grade, 6th month.

Age- and grade-equivalent scores for middle and high school students are less accurate because their skill levels are more variable.

Figure 3-3. Conversion Table: Standard Scores, Scaled or Subtest Scores, and Percentile Ranks

Standard Score	Scaled Score	Percentile Rank
145	19	99
140	18	99
135	17	99
130	16	98
125	15	95
120	14	91
115	13	84
110	12	75
109	–	73
108	–	70
107	–	68
106	–	66
105	11	63
104	–	61
103	–	58
102	–	55
101	–	53
100	10	50
99	–	47
98	–	45
97	–	42
96	–	39
95	9	37
94	–	34
93	–	32
92	–	30
91	–	27
90	8	25
89	–	23
88	–	21
87	–	19
86	–	18
85	7	16
80	6	09
75	5	05
70	4	02
65	3	01
60	2	01
55	1	01

Subtest Scores, Composite Scores, and Index Scores

Your child's test scores may be reported as subtest scores, composite scores, cluster scores, or index scores.

What do I need to know about subtest scores?

Most psychological and educational tests are composed of many subtests. Subtests are short tests that measure different skills and abilities, such as vocabulary, math computation, or short-term memory.

Scaled scores are the mostly commonly used scoring system for subtests. Scaled scores have a Mean of 10 and a Standard Deviation of 3.

What are composite scores, cluster scores, and index scores?

Two or more subtests are often combined into a single score called a composite score, a cluster score, or an index score. Most composite, cluster, and index scores have a mean of 100 and a standard deviation of 15.

Do not rely solely on composite scores to measure your child's skills. Composite scores can mask significant weaknesses. If a child's subtest scores within a composite are very different from each other, the composite score will not accurately measure her skills.

For example, assume your child took a reading test and earned a high score on decoding and a low score on reading comprehension. The composite score on these two subtests is likely to fall in the average range. An average score is misleading because the reading skills are not average.

Measuring Educational Progress

Can I use my child's test scores to track progress?

Maybe. When tracking progress, you need to compare your child's scores from the same edition of the same test. When tracking progress, it is best to use scoring systems that are equal units, such as standard scores. All changes in test scores are not significant. Some differences are accidental.

Can I use age- and grade-equivalent scores to measure my child's progress?

Age- and grade-equivalent scores are one way to estimate progress. If you use age- and grade-equivalent scores, you must compare scores from the same test. Different tests will not measure the same knowledge and skills. You cannot measure your child's progress by comparing age- and grade-equivalent scores on different tests.

Age- and grade-equivalent scores need to be used with caution. These scores are more useful when the tests are given at longer intervals (longer than a year). These scores can tell you if your child made progress, but they cannot tell you how much progress he made.

Never rely on one test or one test score when making decisions about your child's educational programming.

When I looked for scores in my child's evaluation, the results were given as ranges - "average" and "below average." Shouldn't an evaluation report include standard scores and percentile ranks?

Yes! An evaluator should always include standard scores and percentile ranks in evaluation reports. Some evaluators also include raw scores, and age- and grade-equivalent scores. If an evaluation does not include standard scores and percentile ranks, write a letter to the evaluator or the school to request these scores.

My child's evaluation report referred to her skills as "average" although she struggles in school.

Evaluators often describe a child's performance as "average," "above average," or "below average." These labels are arbitrary and are defined by test publishers. Different publishers use different labels for the same scores. For example, a standard score of 85 (16th percentile rank) on a particular test may be "average," "low average," or even "below average," depending on the test publisher.

A child who earns scores in the "average range" may have a disability and require specialized instruction.

If you see large or unexpected changes in your child's test scores, ask the evaluator to check for scoring errors.

What does it mean when a child regresses?

Regression refers to the loss of skills. When a child regresses, scores on the same test drop significantly. If a child's standard scores drop, but the child's age- or grade-equivalent scores increase, this suggests that progress has slowed, but the child did not lose ground.

Regression may also indicate that your child did not master targeted skills. His educational program may not be meeting his needs.

Many children regress over the summer months and during long breaks from school. If you have good baseline data on your child, you can use this data to document regression.

Good data is helpful when you need to request Extended School Year (ESY) services for your child. You can obtain baseline data from criterion-referenced tests, work samples, and from your district's progress monitoring tests (e.g., STAR, AIMSweb).[1]

Learn More about Test Scores and How to Use Test Data

Chapters 10 and 11 in *Wrightslaw: From Emotions to Advocacy, 2nd Edition.*

Available from: www.wrightslaw. com/bks/feta2/feta2.htm

Understanding Your Child's Test Scores CD-ROM (1.5 hrs). Learn about standard scores, percentile ranks, subtest scores, composite or cluster scores, and subtest scatter, how to draw the bell curve, and how to use your child's test scores to create progress graphs.

Available from: www.wrightslaw.com/store/cd.test. scores.htm

Resources

Flanagan, D. P. & Caltabiano, L. (2004). *Test scores: A guide to understanding and using test results.* National Association of School Psychologists. Retrieved from www.nasponline.org/communications/spawareness/testscores.pdf

Salvia, J., Ysseldyke, J.E., & Bolt, S. (2012). *Assessment in special and inclusive education (12th ed.).* Belmont, CA: Wadsworth, Cengage.

Sattler, J. (2008). *Assessment of children: Cognitive Foundations (5th ed.).* San Diego, CA: Author.

Willis, J.O., & Dumont, R. (2002). *Guide to identification of learning disabilities (3rd ed.).* Peterborough, NH: Author.

In Summation

In this chapter, you learned about the bell curve, standard scores, percentile ranks, scaled scores, age-equivalent, and grade-equivalent scores.

As your child's advocate, you need to monitor your child's progress to ensure that it is adequate.

In the next chapter, you will learn about intellectual evaluations and IQ tests.

Endnotes

1. For a list of progress monitoring tests, see www.intensiveintervention.org/chart/progress-monitoring

4 Intellectual Evaluations and IQ Testing

- Developmental and Intellectual Disabilities

- Measuring Intelligence

- Tests of Intelligence

- Nonverbal Tests of Intelligence

- Interpreting Intelligence Tests Results

- Intelligence Tests: Special Factors

If you have concerns about your child's cognitive (intellectual) abilities, an intellectual evaluation can tell you how he is functioning. Intelligence tests are important in establishing realistic expectations of your child's abilities.

In this chapter, you will learn about intellectual disabilities, intelligence, and how intelligence is measured. You will learn about the different types of tests used to measure IQ, and how these tests measure abilities and skills.

When you finish this chapter, you will know why IQ scores change, when you should be concerned about changes in IQ scores, and what you can do.

Developmental and Intellectual Disabilities

Developmental disabilities are severe, chronic disabilities that may be intellectual, physical, or both. The term "intellectual disability" replaced "mental retardation" in common usage and in the *Diagnostic and Statistical Manual of Mental Disorders (DSM-V)*.

If your child has an intellectual disability, she may take longer to learn to speak, walk, and care for her personal needs such as dressing or eating. She may have difficulty solving problems, thinking logically, learning academics and social skills, and communicating.

If you believe that your child may have an intellectual or developmental disability, look for an evaluator who has expertise in evaluating children with these conditions.

My four-year-old has Down syndrome. What do I need to know about evaluating children with intellectual disabilities?

Your child needs a comprehensive assessment that includes tests of intelligence, academic achievement, and adaptive behavior. The evaluator will compare your child's skills to the skills of other children who are the same age.

The evaluation will assess adaptive behavior skills he needs to live independently. Adaptive behavior skills include:

- Daily living skills
- Communication skills
- Social skills

If your child's IQ is in the 70 to 75 range or below and he does not have age-appropriate communication and independent living skills, he will probably be identified as having an intellectual disability.

How will an assessment help?

In addition to assessing your child's intelligence, academics, and adaptive behavior, the evaluation should identify your child's needs in other areas. For example, he may need a speech and language assessment, occupational and physical therapy evaluations, or an assessment to document his need for assistive technology or transition services. A comprehensive battery of evaluations should help in designing an appropriate program for your child.

Although children with intellectual disabilities have complex profiles, most can learn to read and do math.

Measuring Intelligence

Experts do not agree on the definition of intelligence. Some experts believe that intelligence includes strengths and weaknesses. Some view intelligence as a hierarchy of abilities that work together. Others are critical of IQ tests because they do not measure traits like decision-making, judgment, or street smarts.

Intelligence is described as the ability to learn, think, and solve problems. Since different people are good at different types of problem solving, there are different ways to be intelligent.

How do tests measure intelligence?

Intelligence tests measure different skills, including:

- Verbal Reasoning and Vocabulary: thinking with words

- Fluid Reasoning: using language to solve unfamiliar problems

- Visual-Spatial and Visual-Motor Skills: thinking with pictures, designs, and hands

- Short-Term and Working Memory capturing input for temporary storage and manipulating content

- Long-Term Memory Storage and Retrieval: recalling factual information and retrieving it from memory

- Processing Speed: making small decisions quickly with pencil in hand

Your child's overall score on an IQ test is his Full Scale IQ (FSIQ). Different tests use different names for the overall score. On most IQ tests, the mean or average IQ score is 100.

IQ scores between 90 and 110 (25th to 75th percentile) are within the average range. The scores of half of all children (50%) fall between 90 and 110. Twenty-five percent of all children score above 110 and 25% score below 90. If your child obtains a standard score of 75 or lower on an IQ test, he may have an intellectual disability.

If your child has sensory, language, or cognitive impairments, a traditional intelligence test may not accurately reflect his ability to learn. The evaluator may decide to use a specialized intelligence test.

Specialized intelligence tests allow the child to demonstrate his abilities and don't penalize him for his disabilities. Specialized intelligence tests may omit expressive language and/or visual-motor skills. These tests are relatively free of cultural and linguistic bias.

Tests of Intelligence

Wechsler Intelligence Scale for Children, Fourth Edition (WISC-IV)

The *Wechsler Intelligence Scale for Children, Fourth Edition (WISC-IV)*, is the most commonly administered test of ability for children from ages 6 through 16. The *Wechsler Preschool and Primary Scale, Fourth Edition* (WPPSI-IV) is given to children who are ages 2 years, 6 months through 7 years, 7 months. Individuals who are 16 years or older are tested with the *Wechsler Adult Intelligence Test*, Fourth Edition (WAIS-IV).

The *WISC-IV* consists of ten core subtests and five supplementary subtests. The core subtests are used to calculate the Full Scale IQ.

The *WISC-IV* includes four Index scores. These Index scores measure Verbal Comprehension, Perceptual Reasoning, Working Memory, and Processing Speed. (See Table 4-1)

All About Tests and Assessments

Table 4-1. Structure of the *Wechsler Intelligence Scale for Children (WISC-IV)*

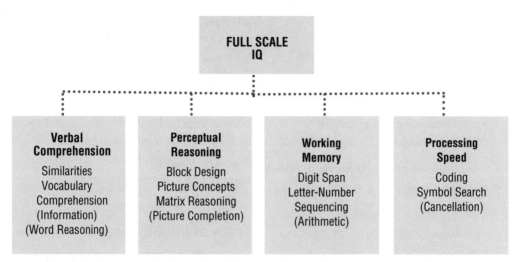

Note: The five subtests within parentheses are supplemental subtests and are not used to calculate the child's Full Scale IQ Score.

The Full Scale IQ score is a measure of general intelligence, scholastic aptitude, and readiness to master school skills. The Full Scale IQ does not measure the non-intellectual traits and abilities needed for academic achievement. No single test measures all abilities needed in these areas. This is one reason your child's scores on different intelligence tests are likely to be different.

If there are significant differences between Index scores or significant differences (scatter) between subtests, the Full Scale IQ **may not** accurately represent your child's level of functioning.

Note: The *WISC-IV* is being revised. The revision process generally takes several years.

Table 4-2. Indexes and Subtests: Wechsler Intelligence Scale for Children-IV (WISC-IV)

Indexes and Subtests	Some of the Abilities Measured
Verbal Comprehension Index	
Similarities	Abstract reasoning, verbal categories and concepts
Vocabulary	Language development, word knowledge, verbal concept formation
Comprehension	Social and practical judgment, common sense
(Information)*	Factual knowledge, long-term memory, recall
(Word Reasoning)*	Verbal comprehension, general reasoning ability
Working Memory Index	
Digit Span	Short-term auditory memory, mental manipulation
Letter Number Sequencing	Sequencing, mental manipulation, attention
(Arithmetic)*	Attention and concentration, numerical reasoning
Perceptual Reasoning Index	
Block Design	Spatial analysis, abstract visual problem-solving
Picture Concepts	Abstract, categorical reasoning
Matrix Reasoning	Pattern recognition, classification, analogical reasoning
(Picture Completion)*	Alertness to detail, visual discrimination
Processing Speed Index	
Coding	Visual-motor coordination, speed, concentration
Symbol Search	Visual-motor quickness, concentration, persistence
(Cancellation)*	Processing speed, visual selective attention, vigilance
*Supplementary subtest not used to calculate FSIQ score.	

What Can We Learn from Sarah's Test Scores?

Sarah is a nine-year-old with a speech and language impairment. Sarah's Full Scale IQ of 89 (23rd percentile) on the *WISC-IV* places her in the Low Average range of intellectual functioning. But Sarah's Full Scale IQ does not accurately describe her strengths and weaknesses.

Look at Sarah's Index scores on the *WISC-IV* in Table 4-3.

Table 4-3. Sarah's Index Scores on the *WISC-IV*

WISC-IV	Standard Score	Percentile Rank
Verbal Comprehension Index	75	05
Working Memory Index	80	09
Perceptual Reasoning Index	106	66
Processing Speed Index	112	79
Full Scale IQ	89	23

Sarah's Verbal Comprehension Index is 75 (5th percentile). Her Working Memory Index is 80 (9th percentile). These scores show that Sarah has significant weaknesses in verbal reasoning and working memory.

But Sarah's Perceptual Reasoning Index, which measures her visual-spatial and visual-motor abilities, is 106 (66th percentile). This means Sarah is good at thinking with pictures and designs. Her Processing Speed Index of 112 (79th percentile) is well above average. She has a good visual memory for abstract symbols. Sarah is fast and accurate with a pencil in hand.

The skills measured by Sarah's Verbal Comprehension and Working Memory Indexes are negatively affected by her speech and language impairment. These scores reflect the impact of Sarah's disability and do not represent her true ability to learn.

Sarah's Perceptual Reasoning Index and Processing Speed Index scores best represent her ability to learn.

The school tested my son with the *Wechsler Intelligence Scale for Children, Fourth Edition*. He received a Full Scale IQ of 65 (1st percentile). His team says that he cannot learn to read. Is this true?

No. Some children with high intelligence have great difficulty learning to read. Other children with intellectual impairments learn to read quite easily.

Your child's progress in learning to read may be slow. Many children with intellectual disabilities require more instruction and practice than their non-disabled peers. Presuming that they can read words, their reading comprehension will depend on their receptive language skills. Language is language whether we hear it through our ears or see it in print.

My child has weaknesses in working memory and processing speed that lowered his Full Scale IQ. The school says that he does not have much potential to learn. Are there tests that would better demonstrate his ability?

Yes. A *WISC-IV* Full Scale IQ is not always appropriate. Several tests measure reasoning ability without direct measures of working memory and processing speed. The *WISC-IV*, for example, can be interpreted in terms of a General Ability Index (GAI) and a Cognitive Proficiency Index (CPI). The GAI measures reasoning ability without the weaknesses (working memory and processing speed) that are often seen in children with learning difficulty. These areas can be looked at separately as part of the CPI.

Differential Ability Scales, Second Edition (DAS-II)

The *Differential Ability Scales, Second Edition (DAS-II)*is designed to measure the skills of children with learning difficulties.

The *DAS-II* is used with children between the ages of 2 years, 6 months and 17 years, 11 months. The test has two overlapping age levels. The evaluator will select the range that is appropriate for a child.

The *DAS-II* includes a General Conceptual Ability (GCA) score (similar to a Full Scale IQ score but with only higher-level conceptual abilities) and three composite scores:

Verbal Cluster Score measures knowledge of words and verbal categories.

Nonverbal Reasoning Cluster Score measures fluid reasoning, pattern recognition, and conceptualization ability.

Spatial Cluster Score measures spatial relations and visual-motor abilities.

The *DAS-II* also provides a Special Nonverbal Composite score that measures problem-solving abilities in children who have weak verbal skills.

The *DAS-II* characterizes memory and processing speed as Diagnostic Subtests. These skills are not included in the General Conceptual Ability (GCA) score. Weaknesses in these areas do not lower the child's score.

Let's look at Sarah's *DAS-II* scores in Table 4-4.

Table 4-4. Sarah's Composite Scores on the *DAS-II*

Differential Ability Scales, Second Edition	Standard Score	Percentile Rank
Verbal Cluster	78	08
Nonverbal Reasoning Cluster	108	70
Spatial Cluster	103	58
Special Nonverbal Composite	107	68
Diagnostic Clusters		
Working Memory	74	04
Processing Speed	115	84

Sarah's core composite scores range from a high of 108 (70th percentile) on the Nonverbal Reasoning Cluster to a low of 78 (8th percentile) on the Verbal Cluster. The General Conceptual Ability (standard score of 96, 39th percentile) has not been provided. According to the *DAS-II* manual, the GCA may not be interpretable given the significant differences between cluster scores[1].

Sarah's Special Nonverbal Composite score of 107 (68th percentile) best represents her ability to learn although her verbal weaknesses will present significant challenges.

On the Diagnostic Clusters, Sarah's Working Memory score of 74 (4th percentile) contrasts with her Processing Speed score of 115 (84th percentile). Sarah makes small decisions with pencil in hand quickly; her working memory is weak.

Woodcock-Johnson Tests of Cognitive Abilities, Third Edition (WJ III COG)

The *WJ III Tests of Cognitive Abilities (WJ III COG)* is a widely used assessment that is designed to measure intelligence. When *Wrightslaw: All About Tests and Assessments* went to press, the *WJ III COG* was being revised and was expected to be available in 2014.

Nonverbal Tests of Intelligence

Nonverbal intelligence tests are designed to measure a child's intellectual functioning without the impact of language. These tests rely heavily on visual-spatial skills, and do not require the child to respond verbally.

If your child has language processing or communication problems, cannot read, or is acquiring the English language, a traditional IQ test may not accurately measure his intellectual ability. If he is assessed with a nonverbal test of intelligence, he is likely to earn higher scores that reflect his actual level of functioning.

My daughter has autism and weak oral language skills. Can we get an accurate picture of her intelligence?

Yes. A test of nonverbal ability will allow your daughter to demonstrate her problem-solving skills without requiring her to speak.

Table 4-5. Some Nonverbal Tests of Intelligence

Test	Description	Age Range
Comprehensive Test of Nonverbal Intelligence, Second Edition (CTONI-2)	Measures analogical reasoning, categorical classification, and sequential reasoning. Child responds by pointing to choices. Caution! Some commentators believe this test may give elevated scores.	6 thru 90
Leiter International Performance Scale, Third Edition (Leiter-3)	Measures intelligence, attention, and neuropsychological abilities. Directions are pantomimed. Child responds by moving objects but it can be adapted to pointing.	3 thru 75+
Naglieri Nonverbal Ability Test, Second Edition (NNAT2)	Measures general reasoning ability with minimal verbal demands. Administered with pencil and paper or by computer	5 thru 17
Primary Test of Nonverbal Intelligence (PTONI)	Measures reasoning abilities with minimal oral directions. Child responds by pointing.	3 thru 9
Test of Nonverbal Intelligence, Fourth Edition (TONI-4)	Reportedly language-free test with directions in Spanish, French, German, Chinese, Vietnamese, Korean, and Tagalog. Child responds by pointing, nodding, or blinking. Caution! Some commentators believe this test may give elevated scores.	6 thru 89

If the school team needs information about her verbal skills, the evaluator can administer tests of language functioning or multiple choice verbal knowledge tests that do not require expressive language skills.

My child has cerebral palsy and is nonverbal. He has difficulty with visual-motor tasks. Can an evaluator measure his IQ?

Yes. Nonverbal tests, including the *Leiter International Performance Scale, Third Edition (Leiter-3)*, and the *Test of Nonverbal Intelligence, Fourth Edition (TONI-4)*, do not

rely on your child's language or motor skills. The directions are modeled. Your child can respond by pointing or by eye gaze.

My 18-year-old is diagnosed with autism and Down syndrome. She reads at the second grade level. Are there tests that can be used to assess a child with severe intellectual disabilities?

If your daughter is like many children on the autism spectrum, the evaluator may decide to use the *Leiter-3*. The block-and-frame format and nonverbal administration of the *Leiter-3* are designed for children with autism and other disabilities. The blocks are light-weight and have rounded corners to minimize safety issues.

Interpreting Intelligence Test Results

What factors affect a child's IQ score?

If your child is not learning to read, his Verbal IQ will drop over time. This drop is called the Matthew Effects.[2]

The Matthew Effects describe the phenomenon where "the rich get richer and the poor get poorer." The Matthew Effects comes from a passage in the New Testament: "For unto every one that hath shall be given, and he shall have abundance: but from him that hath not shall be taken away even that which he hath."[3]

Here is how this works. If your child is a good reader, he will learn by reading. When he reads, his vocabulary increases and he can process more difficult text. The more he reads, the more he will learn.

If your child is a poor reader, he will not learn new words and concepts by reading. He will not acquire background knowledge. Since reading is hard, he will read less than children who are good readers. When he reads less, he will learn less, and the sad cycle continues.

The Matthew Effects: "Reading Affects Everything You Do"

Children who read poorly and/or slowly have difficulty remembering what they read. Reading can be hard and unpleasant. If reading difficulties are allowed to continue, the child's problems will only get worse. Unresolved reading problems have a negative impact on thinking, behavior, and self-concept. Don't delay getting an evaluation!

"Or to put it simply in the words of a tearful nine-year-old, who had fallen frustratingly behind his peers, 'Reading affects everything you do.'" [4]

My child was tested on the same IQ test on two occasions. His IQ score changed. Is this normal?

Yes, it is normal for IQ scores to vary. Tests are not perfect and do not measure skills with absolute consistency. Your child has good days and bad days. This will affect how he performs on tests. A person's cognitive abilities can also change over time.

My child was tested on two IQ tests and earned different scores. Which test should I rely on?

If an evaluator uses a different test, a different edition of a test, or a test that measures different skills, you should expect your child's score to be different. If you want to compare test scores, you must use the same tests, or tests that measure the same things.

If the test includes tasks that are strengths for your child, you can expect your child to earn a higher score on that test. If the test includes tasks that are weaknesses for your child, expect his score to be lower.

Changes in your child's intelligence test scores may be due to:

- Chance

- Lack of effective instruction

- Medical conditions that warrant referrals to specialists

Evaluators make mistakes too. An evaluator may use an incorrect date of birth, calculate the child's age incorrectly, read the wrong table in the test manual, or mistype his results.

If you see unexpected scores, don't be afraid to ask the evaluator to double-check the results.

If your child's IQ score drops significantly, you may want to consult with a neuropsychologist who can examine reasons for the changes. Consider having your child's hearing and vision re-checked.

My child's academic achievement scores are higher than her IQ score. The school says she is outperforming her potential. What does this mean?

On academic achievement tests, half of all children achieve higher than predicted by their IQ scores and half achieve lower. The

term for this is "regression toward the mean." The child's achievement is closer to the Mean (standard score of 100) than the child's IQ score predicts.

Your child cannot outperform her potential. If your child performs better on academic tasks than predicted by an intelligence test, the expectations for her are too low.

As you are learning in *Wrightslaw: All About Tests and Assessments*, different tests measure different skills. Some IQ tests may not accurately measure your child's ability or her true potential.

My child has Down syndrome. The school will not provide speech and language therapy and occupational therapy because his IQ is low. Can a school refuse to provide services because a child has a low IQ score?

No. If your child is like most children with Down syndrome, he needs speech and language therapy and occupational therapy. Speech and language and occupational therapy are related services. The law does not allow schools to use a child's IQ score to deny special education and related services.

When is a score on an intelligence test invalid?

Good testing is not just about scores. If your child's skills are evenly developed, the Full Scale IQ score may provide a good overall picture of her abilities. If your child's skills are not evenly developed, her Full Scale IQ may not be helpful.

For example, if your child is better at thinking with words than thinking with pictures, her Full Scale IQ score may underestimate her abilities and her potential.

When there are large differences between your child's skills (known as scatter), the evaluator may rely more on composite or index scores than on the Full Scale IQ. If differences between composite scores are statistically significant, the examiner should not calculate a Full Scale IQ score.

Intelligence Tests: Special Factors

My child is deaf and uses sign language. We want to understand his cognitive abilities. What do we need to know about evaluations?

There are special factors when evaluating a child who is deaf or hard of hearing.[5] If your child communicates in sign language—not with oral speech—it is not appropriate to use tests of verbal reasoning and knowledge.

Testing should utilize your son's mode of communication, which is sign language. The IDEA requires that tests are "provided and administered in the child's native language or other mode of communication."[6]

The *Leiter-3* is a nonverbal test that assesses intelligence but does not require the child to listen or speak. The examiner teaches the tasks by pantomime and verifies that the child understands the tasks.

If a child is deaf or hard of hearing and uses technologies like high-powered hearing aids or cochlear implants, he may still need to be assessed with nonverbal assessments. It is advisable to consult with professionals who specialize in assessing students who are deaf or hard of hearing. See Chapter 11 to learn about assessments for visual, hearing, and motor skills.

Resources

Kaufman, A.S. (2009). IQ testing 101. New York, NY: Springer.

In Summation

In this chapter, you learned about intellectual disabilities, intelligence, and how intelligence is measured. You learned about different types of tests that are used to measure IQ, and how different tests measure different abilities and skills. You learned that IQ test scores can and do change.

It's time to move on to evaluations of your child's academic and educational skills.

Endnotes

1. Elliot, C.D. (2007). *Differential Ability Scales – Second Edition administration and scoring manual.* San Antonio, TX: Pearson.

2. Stanovich, K. (1986). Matthew effects in reading: Some consequences of individual differences in= the acquisition of literacy. *Reading Research Quarterly*, 21(4), 360-407.

3. Matthew 25:29. Retrieved from http: // biblehub.com/matthew/25-29.htm

4. Stanovich, K. (1986), p.390.

5. 20 U.S.C. §1414(d)(3)(B)

6. 34 C.F.R. §300.304(c)(1)(ii)

5 Academic Achievement Assessments

- Assessments of Reading

- Assessments of Written Language

- Assessments of Mathematics

- Formats of Academic Achievement Tests

In the next chapters, you will learn about the academic achievement tests that measure your child's skills in reading, written language, and mathematics.

Psycho-educational evaluations are used to assess children for learning disabilities, cognitive disabilities, and behavior disorders. These evaluations are also used to identify children who may be eligible for special education services, gifted programs, or other academic assistance.[1] Academic achievement tests are an essential component of a psycho-educational evaluation.

All About Tests and Assessments

A comprehensive evaluation should include tests that measure your child's basic skills, his ability to apply these skills, and his ability to work quickly and efficiently.

The evaluator should observe your child's performance during testing and consider the errors your child made and your child's response style.

Academic achievement tests can also identify risk factors that affect your child's ability to learn. These risk factors include processing difficulties, learning disabilities, and intellectual disabilities.

Assessments of Reading

An assessment of reading needs to focus on your child's ability to recognize individual words and to comprehend text. A comprehensive reading assessment should measure:

- Reading comprehension
- Listening comprehension
- Phonological awareness
- Rapid naming
- Vocabulary
- Fluency
- Word identification
- Word attack
- Spelling
- Alphabet[2]

Tests should be selected so the content and tasks are similar to school reading tasks. Formal and informal assessments may be useful. To learn more about reading assessments, see Chapter 6.

Assessments of Written Language

Writing is an essential part of the school curriculum and is often used to evaluate a child's understanding of concepts. Written language includes three broad areas: written expression, spelling, and handwriting.

A comprehensive written language evaluation should assess your child's skills in these areas:

- Alphabet
- Spelling
- Punctuation and Mechanics
- Writing Sentences
- Writing Paragraphs, Stories, and Essays [3]

A spelling assessment may include standardized, norm-referenced tests, curriculum-based tests, and diagnostic spelling inventories.

A handwriting assessment should include observations of execution, legibility, and speed of writing. If your child prints and writes in cursive, the assessment should include observations of execution, legibility, and speed in both forms of writing. It may also be appropriate to document your child's skills in keyboarding and word processing.

The evaluator should review work samples from the classroom. The specific skills assessed in an assessment of written language will depend on your child's age and unique problems. To learn more about written language assessments, see Chapter 7.

Assessments of Mathematics

An assessment of mathematics should test your child's skills in:

- Math reasoning
- Math computation
- Math fluency

The examiner should supplement norm-referenced tests with criterion-referenced or informal tests to assess your child's mastery of number concepts and math facts.

A math assessment should be structured so it resembles the demands of the classroom. The assessment may include samples of your child's work to identify errors and patterns in the errors. For more about assessments of mathematics, see Chapter 8.

Formats of Academic Achievement Tests

The academic tests described in these chapters are administered individually. An academic test can assess multiple subjects or a single subject.

Multiple-subject tests provide information about your child's academic skills in reading, writing, and mathematics.

Some multiple-subject tests assess other skills including oral language, fluency, rapid naming, and phonological awareness.

Multiple-subject achievement tests include:

- *Kaufman Test of Educational Achievement, Second Edition (KTEA-II)*
- *Wechsler Individual Achievement Test, Third Edition (WIAT-III)*
- *Woodcock-Johnson III Tests of Achievement (WJ III ACH)*

Multiple-subject tests have limitations. These tests do not have to be administered in their entirety. The examiner may choose the subtests she wants to use. To do a comprehensive evaluation on your child, the examiner often needs to supplement a multiple-subject test with additional tests and subtests to measure specific areas.

Single-subject achievement tests often provide more information about your child's strengths and weaknesses in one academic area.

Examples of single-subject tests include:

- *Gray Oral Reading Tests, Fifth Edition (GORT-5)*
- *Comprehensive Test of Phonological Processing, Second Edition (CTOPP2)*
- *Oral and Written Language Scales, Second Edition (OWLS-II)*
- *Test of Written Language, Fourth Edition (TOWL-4)*
- *KeyMath-3 Diagnostic Assessment (KeyMath-3)*

Resources

International Dyslexia Association. (n.d.). *Testing and Evaluation*. Retrieved from: www.interdys.org/ewebeditpro5/upload/TestingandEvaluation.pdf

Horowitz, S.H. (n.d.). *Types of Tests to Assess Learning Disabilities and Related Disorders*. Retrieved from: www.ncld.org/parents-child-disabilities/ld-testing/types-learning-disabilities-tests

The International Dyslexia Association: www.interdys.org

The Florida Center for Reading Research: www.fcrr.org

In the next chapter, you will learn how reading is assessed. You will learn about reading skills, tests that are used to measure reading skills, and answers to frequently asked questions about reading tests.

Endnotes

1. Sattler, J.M. (1992). *Assessment of Children, 3rd ed.* Jerome M. Sattler, Publisher: San Diego, CA

2. Farrall, M. (2012). *Reading assessment: Linking language, literacy, and cognition.* John Wiley & Sons: Hoboken, NJ

3. Farrall, M. (2013). The assessment of written syntax. *Perspectives on Language and Literacy.* 38(3), 31-36

In Summation

In this chapter, you learned that psycho-educational evaluations include academic achievement tests. These tests measure your child's basic skills in reading, written language, and mathematics, his ability to apply these skills, and to work quickly and efficiently.

Reading Assessments

- Assessing Reading Difficulties and Disabilities

- Reading Skills

- Tests That Measure Reading

- Answers to Questions About Reading Tests

- Assessing Reading: Special Factors

In this chapter, you will learn about reading difficulties and disabilities, such as dyslexia, and how reading is assessed. You will learn about reading skills, tests that are used to measure reading skills, and answers to frequently asked questions about reading tests.

Reading is the gateway skill to learning. In third grade, the focus of your child's education changes from learning to read to reading to learn. Your child will use reading skills to learn history, science, geography, literature, math, and other subjects in the curriculum.

If your child has not learned to read by the end of third grade, he will be in trouble. He will not be able to learn independently from books. He will not understand what the teachers write on the board. He will not be able to write reports and essays. He will fall further behind his classmates. If he is like most children with reading problems, he will not catch up unless he receives a well-designed, research-based intervention.

There are many reasons why children do not read fluently by third grade. If you suspect that your child has reading difficulties or a reading disability, get an evaluation now. Do not delay. A reading assessment is the first step in identifying your child's problems and developing solutions so he can improve his reading.

Children Who Are Poor Readers in 3rd Grade Do Not Catch Up

"75% of children who were poor readers in the 3rd grade remained poor readers in the 9th grade and could not read well when they became adults."

–Joseph Torgeson in *Catch Them Before They Fall*

www.aft.org/pdfs/americaneducator/ springsummer1998/torgesen.pdf

---

Assessing Reading Difficulties and Disabilities

A comprehensive reading assessment should measure your child's decoding and receptive language skills.

The decoding part of the evaluation should include tests of:

- Alphabet
- Word identification (word recognition)
- Word attack (phonics)
- Spelling
- Fluency (rate and accuracy)
- Passage comprehension

The receptive language portion should include tests that measure listening comprehension and vocabulary. Listening comprehension tests measure how well your child understands language. These tests can alert you to receptive language problems that affect reading comprehension.

Weaknesses in phonological processing skills are the leading cause of reading disabilities. A comprehensive reading assessment should include tests that measure:

- Phonological/phonemic awareness
- Phonological memory
- Rapid naming

If your child has a history of speech and language problems or you suspect that he has a language problem, a comprehensive reading assessment should include a speech and language assessment.[1]

Your child's hearing and vision should be checked. It is important to rule out problems with visual acuity. Most reading difficulties are not caused by vision problems and cannot be corrected by vision-related therapies.

The school wants to do an informal reading assessment on my child. What is an informal reading assessment?

An informal reading assessment may be a teacher-made test or an informal reading inventory (IRI). It can also be the end of the unit test from the reading program that is used with all the students.

Teacher-made tests are based on the curriculum and prepared by teachers. Teachers use scores to measure their students' progress.

Informal reading inventories include graded word lists, graded passages, and comprehension questions for the passages. Informal reading inventories usually classify four levels of reading skill:

1. Independent level: The child reads without assistance.

2. Instructional level: The child finds the material challenging, not too hard or too easy.

3. Frustration level: The child is frustrated when trying to understand what he reads.

4. Listening capacity or potential level: The child understands material that is read to him.

An informal reading inventory **may not be used** to determine if a child is eligible for special education or in other high-stakes education decisions.

The school wants to do a screening test of my child's reading. What is a screening test?

A screening test is a brief assessment that is intended to identify children who are at risk for educational or learning problems. Screening tests are limited and **may not** identify a child's problems that need to be evaluated. Screening tests should **never** be used in place of a comprehensive evaluation.[2]

Who can evaluate my child's reading skills?

Reading specialists, learning disability specialists, special educators, speech and language pathologists, clinical psychologists, and school psychologists evaluate reading skills.

Can you test a child for dyslexia?

Yes. Dyslexia is a specific learning disability that affects language.

A child with dyslexia will have difficulty reading accurately and fluently. Spelling will be poor. Most children with dyslexia have weaknesses in phonological processing.[3] Many also have weaknesses in rapid naming.

All About Tests and Assessments

Most standardized, norm-referenced tests that are used to test for learning disabilities are also used to evaluate children for dyslexia.

Reading Skills

No test measures all reading skills. Different tests measure different skills. Reading skills include:

Letters (LTRS): Child identifies letters names and sounds, or points to letters in response to letter names or sounds.

Phonological Awareness (PA): Phonemic awareness is an umbrella term that refers to the awareness of individual sounds in words. It includes skills at the word, syllable, and individual sound level. This skill serves as the foundation for learning to read.

In tests of phonological awareness the child rhymes words, segments sounds in words, blends sounds, and identifies sounds. The ability to perceive and manipulate individual sounds is most important.

Rapid Automatic Naming (RAN): Child names colors, objects, letters, or numbers in series. Letter naming is the most important skill for reading.

Letter &Word Identification (L/W ID): Child recognizes regular and irregular words in a list. Younger children and poor readers recognize letters.

Word Attack (WA): Child recognizes nonsense words. Nonsense words are made-up words that assess skill with phonics.

Reading Vocabulary (RV): Child provides antonyms, synonyms, or complete analogies in response to written words.

Reading Comprehension (RC): Child answers open-ended or multiple-choice questions, points to pictures, or fills in missing words. Different methods for assessing comprehension may result in different scores, depending on the child's profile.

Fluency and Automaticity (FL/AU): Child reads passages aloud while being timed. Tests of automaticity and accuracy require the child to read real words and/or nonsense words while being timed.

Listening Comprehension (LC):
Child answers questions based on passages that are read to him. LC can provide important information about comprehension difficulties.

Tests That Measure Reading

Your child's reading should be assessed by tests that measure specific skills. Achievement tests can assess multiple subjects or a single subject. Frequently used multiple-subject achievement tests used to assess reading skills include:

- *Kaufman Test of Educational Achievement, Second Edition (KTEA-II)*

- *Wechsler Individual Achievement Test, Third Edition (WIAT-III)*

- *Woodcock-Johnson III Tests of Achievement (WJ III ACH)*

The *Kaufman Test of Educational Achievement, Second Edition (KTEA-II)* provides valuable information about phonological awareness, oral fluency, and reading fluency. The oral language subtests are not a substitute for a speech and language evaluation. Check Table 6-1 for the reading skills measured by the *KTEA-II*.

In addition to composite and subtest scores, the *KTEA-II* provides an error analysis that is useful in planning direct, explicit systematic instruction. Composite scores should be viewed with caution when there are large differences between subtest scores. You should always be provided with subtest scores.

The *KTEA-II* is under revision. You will find additional information and updates at www.pearsonassessments.com.

The *Wechsler Individual Achievement Test, Third Edition (WIAT-III)* measures the reading skills checked in Table 6-1. The *WIAT-III* oral language subtest results should be interpreted with caution. They are not a substitute for a comprehensive evaluation of receptive and expressive language skills.

The *WIAT-III* has an unusual way of scoring the reading comprehension test for children who read significantly below grade level. If your child is a poor reader but his score on the *WIAT-III* reading comprehension test is high, ask the evaluator whether he was dropped back to below grade-level passages. Sometimes children earn high scores because they are not actually reading grade-level text. The *WIAT-III* may be scored by computer or by hand.

Many evaluators use the *WIAT-III* together with the Wechsler tests of intelligence so they can compare ability and achievement. See Chapter 4 for information about the Wechsler and other tests of intelligence. Additional information about the Wechsler tests is available at www.psychcorp.come

The *Woodcock-Johnson III Tests of Achievement (WJ III ACH)* include a standard battery and an extended battery. See Table 6-1 for the skills measured by these batteries. The *WJ III* includes other supplemental subtests.

The *WJ III* is scored by computer and cannot be scored by hand. Because scoring tables are not provided, it is difficult for an evaluator to verify the accuracy of scores obtained. If you have questions about the accuracy of your child's scores, ask the evaluator to double check the raw scores on the protocol and as typed into the scoring program.

The *WJ III* subtests are organized into clusters. If there are significant differences between your child's subtest scores, you should view the cluster scores with caution. Because the subtests are short, they may not provide sufficient information about what your child knows and is ready to learn.

The *WJ III* written expression subtests should always be supplemented by writing tests that require longer writing samples. The Passage Comprehension subtest should be supplemented by reading tests that use longer passages.

The *WJ III* is under revision. Updates and more information is available at www. riversidepublishing.com.

Single-subject reading tests often provide more information about your child's strengths and weaknesses. Commonly used single-subject reading tests include:

- *Comprehensive Test of Phonological Processing, Second Edition (CTOPP2)*

- *Test of Word Reading Efficiency, Second Edition (TOWRE-2)*

- *Gray Oral Reading Tests, Fifth Edition (GORT-5)*

- *Test of Silent Word Reading Fluency (TOSWRF)*

Tests That Measure Phonological Processing

The *Comprehensive Test of Phonological Processing, Second Edition (CTOPP2)* is the gold standard for phonological processing. The *CTOPP2* measures the skills that make reading and spelling possible. Assessing these skills makes it possible to understand why a child has difficulty reading and how to design his instruction.

The *CTOPP2* measures three areas of phonological processing:

Phonological memory is where speech sounds are held before they are processed. It is important for learning decoding, spelling, and vocabulary.

Phonological awareness refers to the awareness of speech sounds. It is the prerequisite skill for learning phonics. A child who has a weakness in phonological awareness is often described as having dyslexia.

Rapid naming is the ability to name objects, colors, letters, and numbers aloud quickly while being timed. This is important for reading with fluency.

Tests That Measure Reading Fluency and Comprehension

Fluency (rate and accuracy) is essential for reading comprehension. Children who read slowly take longer to complete assignments and they remember less.

The *Test of Word Reading Efficiency, Second Edition (TOWRE-2)* measures the child's ability to recognize real and nonsense words in a list format with accuracy and automaticity. The *TOWRE-2* can help differentiate between different types of reading deficits and can be used to measure progress.

The *Test of Silent Word Reading Fluency (TOSWRF)* measures reading fluency. The child reads words printed without spaces and makes slash marks between the words while being timed. The *TOSWRF* is not designed to measure reading comprehension. This test is not appropriate for a child who has difficulty controlling his pencil.

The *Gray Oral Reading Tests, Fifth Edition (GORT-5),* measure reading fluency and comprehension. The child answers questions based on passages that he reads aloud. The *GORT-5* measures oral reading rate, accuracy, fluency, and comprehension. It also provides an Oral Reading Index, a combined measure of fluency and comprehension.

As you review the skills measured by reading tests in Table 6-1, you will see that no reading test measures all reading skills. To understand what your child's test scores mean, you need to know what skills the test measured. A test that measures many skills may not be better than a test that measures fewer skills well.

Answers to Questions About Reading Tests

My first-grader's scores on the reading subtests of the *Woodcock-Johnson III Tests of Achievement* were below average. I am concerned but his teacher says he will read when he is ready. Do reading test scores improve when a child matures?

You are right to be concerned. If your son's reading subtest scores are below average in first grade, he has a problem. Reading problems are not caused by immaturity and cannot be outgrown. The notion that children who are late bloomers in reading will catch up when they get older is a myth.[5]

You need to get a comprehensive reading assessment. Tests that measure your child's phonological processing, phonics skills, and spelling will clarify why your child is having difficulty and what skills need to be addressed.

On the *Woodcock-Johnson III*, my child scored much higher on the Letter & Word Identification subtest than on the Word Attack subtest. What do these scores mean?

Good question! The difference in these subtest scores is important. The Letter & Word Identification subtest measures your child's ability to read regular and irregular words. The Word Attack subtest measures her ability to apply the rules of phonics to unfamiliar words (nonsense words).

The differences in her subtest scores may mean that she learned to read by sight and did not learn the rules of phonics. She does not know how to break large words into syllables to sound them out.

She is likely to have trouble when she reaches third or fourth grade. Because she does not

All About Tests and Assessments

Table 6-1. Reading Tests and the Skills They Measure

Test	LTRS	PA	RAN	L/W ID	WA	RV	RC	FL/AU	LC
Comprehensive Test of Phonological Processing, Second Edition (CTOPP2)**		√	√						
Gray Diagnostic Reading Tests, Second Edition (GDRT-2)		√	√	√		√	Age 8 & above		√
Gray Oral Reading Tests, Fifth Edition (GORT-5)							√	√	
Kaufman Test of Educational Achievement, Second Edition (KTEA-II)		√	√	√	√		MP & OE	√	√
Lindamood Auditory Conceptualization Test, Third Edition (LAC-3)		√							
Phonological Awareness Test, Second Edition (PAT2)		√		√	√				
Test of Phonological Awareness, Second Edition:Plus (TOPA-2+)		√		√					
Test of Reading Comprehension, Fourth Edition (TORC-4)						√	MC	√	
Test of Silent Contextual Reading Fluency, Second Edition (TOSCRF-2)								√	
Test of Silent Word Reading Fluency, Second Edition (TOSWRF-2)								√	
Test of Word Reading Efficiency, Second Edition (TOWRE2)								√	
Wechsler Individual Achievement Test, Third Edition (WIAT-III)				√	√		OE	√	√
Woodcock-Johnson III Tests of Achievement (WJ III ACH)	√	√	√	√	√	√	FB	√	√
Woodcock Reading Mastery Test, Third Edition (WRMT-3)**		√	√	√	√	√	FB	√	√
Word Identification and Spelling Test (WIST)				√	√				

Key: Letters (LTRS), Phonological Awareness (PA), Rapid Automatic Naming (RAN), Letter Word ID (L/W ID), Word Attack (WA), Reading Vocabulary (RV), Reading Comprehension (RC), Fluency and Automaticity (FL/AU), Listening Comprehension (LC). **Formats:** OE = Open Ended. FB=Fill in blank MC= Multiple Choice ** **May give elevated scores**

know the rules of phonics, she will not have the tools she needs to recognize new words.

No research supports using sight word instruction when teaching a child to read.[6] You want your child to be an independent reader. Before she can be an independent reader, she must learn how letters represent the sounds of the English language.

My child is in second grade but he hasn't learned to read. His score on the Passage Comprehension subtest of the *Woodcock-Johnson III* was in the average range. How can he get an average score when he can't read?

Some subtests, including the Passage Comprehension subtest, include questions that use pictures as clues. Young children often use the pictures to guess the correct answers and boost their scores. Good readers do not use pictures and they do not have to guess.

Ask your son's evaluator to test his skills in word identification, word attack (nonsense words), and reading fluency. Ask the evaluator to use a reading comprehension test that does not provide pictures. Recognizing pictures is **not** a valid measure of reading comprehension.

My daughter reads slowly and inaccurately. On the *Gray Oral Reading Tests, Fifth Edition (GORT-5)*, her Comprehension score was average, but her fluency was well

below average. I'm confused. Her reading skills are not average. How can she earn an average score?

Many young children use their thinking skills to answer questions on tests when they cannot read the material. For example, when asked this question, "When did Johnny eat breakfast?" most children answer the question correctly without reading the text.

Your child's ability to use thinking skills cannot compensate for her poor word recognition skills. She cannot guess her way through a biology or history text.

My son is in the first grade. He struggles to read. How can his scores on the *Standardized Reading Inventory, Second Edition* be in the average range?

Many reading tests do not accurately measure a first-grader's skills. A reading test may provide scores that overestimate the child's true ability.

If you think a test did not accurately measure your child's skills, ask the evaluator if the test had enough items to measure the skills of your young child - this is called the test floor. Ask the evaluator if your child would benefit by more in-depth diagnostic testing.

Progress monitoring tools designed to measure the performance of young children are useful in measuring the reading skills of young children. For more information about progress monitoring, see Chapter 10 about

All About Tests and Assessments

Evaluations of Specific Learning Disabilities and Attention-Deficit/Hyperactivity Disorders (ADHD).

My child has an IQ of 75 (5th percentile). On reading tests, he earns scores in the 70s. His team says that is the best we can expect. Is this true?

No. Learning to read is not primarily a function of intelligence.[7] Some children with low IQs learn to decode text easily. Others have great difficulty. The ease or difficulty of learning to decode text depends, for the most part, on phonological awareness.

If your child has an intellectual disability, a comprehensive reading assessment can identify his strengths, weaknesses, and what he needs in an effective reading instructional program. His progress may be slow. He may need more direct, explicit instruction in vocabulary, verbal reasoning, and inferential thinking to understand what he reads.

Assessing Reading: Special Factors

My child has autism. What do we need to know about evaluating his reading?

As you know, children with autism have a broad range of skills. Some children with autism have severe communication deficits. Others struggle with social skills and pragmatics.

If your child is verbal, he should have the same skills tested as a typical child. If he has difficulty decoding, this is usually due to weaknesses in phonemic awareness and/or rapid naming so these skills need to be assessed.

Consult with your evaluator about your child's oral language skills and whether he needs additional testing in this area.

My child is nonverbal. Can his reading be assessed?

Yes. Some tests of reading do not require the child to speak. In Table 6-2, you will find a list of tests and subtests that measure reading skills in children who are nonverbal.

My daughter has a history of ear infections and language delays. She is struggling to learn the alphabet. Should I have her tested?

Yes. Language delays, ear infections, and difficulty learning the alphabet are factors that put your child at risk for reading problems. You need to begin screening and monitoring her reading skills when she is in kindergarten.

Your child may benefit from an evaluation by an Audiologist to check for a Central Auditory Processing Disorder.

Progress monitoring tools, including *AIMSweb* and *DIBELS-N* are used to monitor the development of reading skills. If reading problems are identified early, your child's teachers can make sure that she achieves and maintains grade-level reading skills.

Table 6-2. Tests That Measure Reading Skills in Nonverbal Children

Test	Subtest	Skill
Lindamood Auditory Conceptualization Test, Third Edition (LAC-3)		Phonemic Awareness
Test of Reading Comprehension, Fourth Edition (TORC-4)	Relational Vocabulary	Reading Vocabulary
Diagnostic Assessment of Reading, Second Edition (DAR-2)	DAR-2 Silent Reading Comprehension (grades 3+)	Reading Comprehension
Gray Silent Reading Tests (GSRT)		Reading Comprehension
Test of Reading Comprehension, Fourth Edition (TORC-4)	Sentence Completion, Paragraph Construction, Text Comprehension	Sentence Comprehension Sentence Comprehension & Sequencing Reading Comprehension
Test of Reading Comprehension, Fourth Edition (TORC-4)	Contextual Fluency	Reading Fluency These tests measure fluency; they do not measure accuracy.
Test of Silent Contextual Reading Fluency, Second Edition (TOSCRF-2)		
Test of Silent Reading Efficiency and Comprehension (TOSREC)		
Test of Silent Word Reading Fluency, Second Edition (TOSWRF-2)		
Woodcock-Johnson III Tests of Achievement (WJ III)	Reading Fluency	
Any test of spelling will provide information about a child's skill with phonics.		Spelling/Orthography
Test of Orthographic Competence (TOC)		Knowledge of letters, abbreviations, punctuation, and spelling

Resources

Early Warning! Why Reading by the End of Third Grade Matters. Retrieved from www.ccf.ny.gov/KidsCount/kcResources/AECFReporReadingGrade3.pdf

Dyslexia Basics Fact Sheet. Retrieved from www.interdys.org/ewebeditpro5/upload/DyslexiaBasicsREVMay2012.pdf

Is My Child Dyslexic? Common characteristics of dyslexia and related learning disorders. Retrieved from www.interdys.org/ewebeditpro5/upload/IsMyChildDyslexic.pdf

Understanding Your Dyslexia. Retrieved from www.interdys.org/ewebeditpro5/upload/UnderstandingYourDyslexia.pdf

Farrall, M. (2008) *Reading Tests: What They Measure and Don't Measure.* Retrieved from Wrightslaw at www.wrightslaw.com/info/test.read.farrall.htm

The International Dyslexia Association: www.interdys.org

The Florida Center for Reading Research:www.fcrr.org

University of Oregon DIBELS Data System: https://dibels.uoregon.edu/

In Summation

Reading is the most important skill taught in school and learned by children. Your goal is to ensure that your child learns to read independently by the end of third grade. If she does not learn to read by the end of third grade, she can learn to read later, but it will require more work.

If your child struggles with reading, get a comprehensive assessment to identify the causes of her difficulties and research-based approaches to remediation now.

In this chapter, you learned about tests and assessments that identify reasons why children struggle with reading. Writing goes hand in hand with reading.

In the next chapter, you will learn about tests of written language. You will learn about assessments used to identify written language problems, including spelling and handwriting.

Endnotes

1. Farrall, M. (2012). *Reading assessment: Linking language, literacy, and cognition.* John Wiley & Sons: Hoboken, NJ

2. 20 U.S.C. §1414(a)(1)(E)

3. The International Dyslexia Association. (2002, November). *What Is Dyslexia?* Retrieved from: www.interdys.org/FAQWhatIs.htm

4. 20 U.S.C. §1401(30), 34 C.F.R. §300.8(c)(10)

5. Lyon, R. (1999). *The NICHD research program in reading development, reading disorders, and reading instruction.* Retrieved from www.bartonreading.com/pages/keys99_nichd.cfm.html

6. Farrall, M. (2012)

7. National Institutes of Health. (2011, November). *NIH-funded study finds dyslexia not tied to IQ.* Retrieved from www.nih.gov/news/health/nov2011/nichd-03.htm

7 Writing and Spelling Assessments

- Assessing Written Language Difficulties and Disabilities

- Written Language Skills

- Tests That Measure Written Language

- Answers to Questions About Written Language Tests

In this chapter, you will learn about written language and how written language is assessed. You will learn about writing and spelling skills, tests that are used to measure written language skills, and answers to frequently asked questions about test results.

Writing is hard. When your child puts pen to paper, he must use the rules for grammar, spelling, and mechanics. He must plan, organize, and revise what he has to say. His skills in language, spatial thinking, attention, memory, processing speed, and handwriting must work together.

All About Tests and Assessments

Writing is not just about putting words on paper. Your child will use writing to communicate and to learn. When he writes about science, history, and literature, the act of writing will help him learn these subjects.

If your child has difficulty writing and spelling, he is likely to have difficulty across the curriculum. You need to recognize the problems that signal a difficulty or disability in written language.

Monitor your child's writing skills from kindergarten through high school. The teachers can provide more effective remediation in written language if they implement it early and target your child's specific, unique needs.

Assessing Written Language Difficulties and Disabilities

Different children have different types of writing problems. Some children can write sentences but cannot write paragraphs or essays. Some struggle to express their thoughts in sentences. Others have handwriting problems that make it difficult to focus on what they want to say.

Many children have weaknesses in more than one area of written expression. A comprehensive written language evaluation should identify your child's strengths and weaknesses related to all areas of written expression.

My child struggles with writing and spelling. He needs to be evaluated.

What should an assessment of written language include?

The skills assessed in a comprehensive written language evaluation will depend on your child's age and unique problems. A comprehensive written language evaluation should assess these skills:

- Alphabet Knowledge

- Spelling

- Mechanics (Capitalization and Punctuation)

- Sentence Writing

- Paragraph and Story Writing

- Writing Fluency

- Handwriting and/or Keyboarding

- Essay and Report Writing [1]

The evaluator should also review writing samples from the classroom.

My child has struggled with writing since first grade. Are there risk factors for problems with written expression?

Yes. If your child has reading problems, he is likely to have writing problems. Risk factors for writing problems include difficulty learning the alphabet, poor handwriting, and weak expressive language skill. [2]

If your child has a poor vocabulary, difficulty writing sentences, or difficulty organizing his thoughts, you need to get a written language assessment.

Table 7-1. Warning Signs of Written Language Problems

Source: The National Council on Learning Disabilities[3]

Young Children	Children in School	Older Children & Adults
• Avoids coloring and writing tasks • Difficulty holding the pencil • Laborious letter formation and irregular spacing • Letters are not on the line • Difficulty writing the alphabet • Complains "my hand hurts"	• Awkward or illegible handwriting • Writing is laborious • Mixture of lower and upper case letters to avoid reversals • Poor spelling • Writes bare-bone sentences • Writes sentences that have the same structure • Sentences lack grammar • Has trouble thinking of what to say or write • May procrastinate when asked to write	• Inefficient handwriting • Poor spelling • Difficulty with grammar and sentence structure • Few or no transition words • Difficulty organizing thoughts and writing paragraphs • Difficulty completing writing tasks on time • Avoids writing book reports and essays

When should we have our child evaluated for written language problems?

If your child is at risk for writing problems, you can have him tested in kindergarten. At that young age, an assessment should focus on handwriting and alphabet skills. The evaluator should also look at classroom writing samples.

Warning! Many norm-referenced tests of written expression are not sufficiently sensitive to accurately identify writing problems in young children.

When assessing the skills of young children, the evaluator should examine the child's functional performance in the classroom.

Share work samples with the evaluator and team meetings.

My child's written work is full of spelling errors. What causes spelling problems? Can her spelling problems be assessed?

Spelling is an important component of written expression. Poor spellers often rely on simple one-syllable words so it is difficult or impossible for them to express what they need to say in writing. Many poor spellers are afraid to take risks.[4]

Spelling should always be tested when there are concerns about reading and writing.

All About Tests and Assessments

Spelling problems, like reading problems, are caused by weaknesses in language-based skills. Poor spellers have difficulty discriminating the sounds (phonemes) and meaningful parts of words. Some poor spellers also have difficulty with handwriting and with visualizing how words should look on paper.

How is spelling assessed?

The evaluator can assess spelling with standardized norm-referenced tests and subtests, and with diagnostic spelling inventories.

Spelling tests and inventories are lists of words that range from easy (individual letters) to complex (multi-syllable words). The evaluator analyzes your child's spelling errors to determine her developmental stage as a speller and to identify the skills that need to be addressed to improve her spelling.

Are there tests of handwriting?

Yes, but handwriting tests are limited in reliability and/or validity. The best way to test handwriting is to look at handwriting samples. When you look at handwriting samples, you see that some children make oversized letters. Others do not orient their letters to the line. Letter strokes are distorted and out of sequence.

If your child's handwriting samples are hard to read, this suggests that he needs direct instruction or assistive technology.

If your child writes slowly and with great effort, he needs a more efficient writing system. If your child needs to focus on how to hold a pencil, it will be hard for him to write well.

My child's handwriting is completely illegible. How do you assess illegible handwriting?

Any assessment of handwriting should include observations of execution, legibility, and speed of writing.

Execution refers to correct and consistent pencil hold, posture, and letter formation. Problems that impede a child's progress in handwriting are not always apparent when looking at writing samples. Observations provide essential information. For example, a young child may "draw" a letter such as "m" using separate strokes, starting on the right side of the letter.

Legibility involves the readability of letters, and spacing within and between words.

If your child has learned manuscript and cursive, the assessment should consider the execution, legibility, and speed of both forms of writing.[5] Speed is increasingly important as your child moves beyond the early grades.

Since your child has poor handwriting, he should be evaluated to determine his needs for occupational therapy and assistive technology.

After my child had a written language assessment, the evaluator recommended that he have a speech and language evaluation. What is the connection?

The deficits that affect your child's oral language skills will also affect his ability to express his thoughts on paper. This is why he needs an assessment of expressive language. See Chapter 9 for more information about speech and language testing.

My son has weak oral language skills. He cannot easily communicate what he wants to say. His expressive language scores are below average. Will he have difficulty with written language too?

Most likely, yes. Written language skills are built on oral language skills. If your child has weak oral language skills, he will find it hard to write a story, a summary, or an essay.

A child who has poor word retrieval, grammar, or syntax will find it difficult to write well-formed phrases and clauses. This child will struggle to write in the correct tense and with noun/verb agreement. It will be hard to write sentences that flow with logic and sequence.

What is dysgraphia?

Dysgraphia is a specific learning disability that affects writing.

If your child has dysgraphia, writing down his thoughts will be difficult. He is likely to have trouble with handwriting, spelling, and putting thoughts on paper. Poor penmanship is not the same thing as dysgraphia. It can, however, be part of having dysgraphia.

Written Language Skills

Different tests of written language measure different skills. Written language skills include:

Alphabet: A standard set of letters that represent sounds (phonemes) in language.

Spelling: Use of alphabetic letters to write words. Good spellers write with a better vocabulary than poor spellers.

Punctuation: Symbols that indicate the structure and organization of written language (e.g., periods, commas, colons, semicolons, and quotation marks).

Mechanics: A general term that refers to spelling, punctuation, and capitalization.

Sentence: Words grouped to express a statement, question, or request that begins with a capital letter and ends with a punctuation mark.

Paragraph: A unit of written expression that includes one or more sentences about an idea or topic.

Tests That Measure Written Language

Your child's test scores do not tell the whole story. Small differences between tests can result in large differences in scores.

When you read an evaluation of written expression, pay close attention to the skills measured by each test.

Woodcock-Johnson III Tests of Achievement (WJ III)

The *WJ III* subtests in written expression include:

- **Writing Samples** measure the ability to write sentences. The child is not penalized for errors in grammar, spelling, or punctuation.

- **Writing Fluency** measures skill in formulating simple sentences quickly. To receive credit, the child writes sentences using three target words. He is not penalized for awkward sentences, spelling, punctuation, capitalization, or handwriting.

- **Editing** examines skill in identifying and correcting errors in punctuation, capitalization, spelling, and word usage.

The *WJ III* only measures the child's ability to write sentences so it should not be used as the only measure of writing skill.

Kaufman Test of Educational Achievement, Second Edition (KTEA-II)

On the *KTEA-II,* the Written Expression subtest uses a story format. The examiner selects a level based on the child's age and skill.

A young child prints letters, writes words, and writes a dictated sentence. An older child edits passages for errors in capitalization and punctuation. He writes sentences to go with the story and combine facts into compound and complex sentences. At the end, he writes a summary of the story.

Scoring for the summary is based on length, content, sentence structure, and organization. Sentences in the summary that do not make sense or are grammatically incorrect may not affect the child's score significantly. Spelling is measured on a separate subtest and does not count on the Written Expression subtest.

Oral and Written Language Scales, Second Edition (OWLS-II)

The *OWLS-II Written Expression Scale* has five levels that are selected to match a child's age or skill. The skills measured in the different levels vary in complexity.

Young children print letters, write words, and dictate sentences. Older children write sentences for different purposes, fill in missing words, add prefixes and suffixes to words, combine facts into sentences, write paragraphs, and write a summary of an orally presented story.

The *OWLS-II* is scored for spelling and mechanics. It provides an error analysis that is helpful for instructional planning. The *OWLS-II* also offers scales for Listening Comprehension, Oral Expression, and Reading Comprehension.

Table 7-2. Written Language Tests and the Skills They Measure

Test/Subtest	Alphabet	Spelling	Punctuation & Mechanics	Sentences	Paragraphs, Stories, & Essays
Assessment of Literacy & Language (ALL)	√	Invented Spelling			
Kaufman Test of Educational Achievement, Second Edition (KTEA-II)	√	Spelling is scored on separate subtest	√	√	√
Oral and Written Language Scales, Second Edition (OWLS-II)	√	√	√	√	√
Process Assessment of the Learner, Second Edition (PAL-II)	√			√	Compositional fluency, note taking, report writing
Test of Written Language, Fourth Edition (TOWL-4)		√	√	√	√
Wechsler Individual Achievement Test, Third Edition (WIAT-III)	√	Spelling is assessed on separate subtest	Scored on Sentence Comp. Essay is only scored for spelling with correct word sequences	√	√
Woodcock-Johnson III Tests of Achievement (WJ III)	Small sample of letters assessed in spelling subtest	Assessed in separate subtests	Assessed primarily in separate subtest	√	

Test of Written Language, Fourth Edition (TOWL-4)

The *TOWL-4* focuses on two areas. One area consists of subtests that measure the child's ability to:

- Write dictated sentences with correct spelling, punctuation, and capitalization

- Read and use words in sentences

- Combine sentences

- Edit nonsensical sentences to make sense

The *TOWL-4* also assesses the child's ability to write a story based upon a picture prompt while being timed. Some evaluators feel that the picture prompts are young in content. This test is likely to provide inflated scores for older children.

Wechsler Individual Achievement Test, Third Edition (WIAT-III)

The *WIAT-III* measures three areas of written expression:

- Alphabet Writing Fluency

- Sentence Composition

- Essay Composition

Alphabet Writing Fluency measures the number of unique and legible letters written by the child within 30 seconds.

Sentence Composition requires the child to use specific words and combine facts into sentences. Responses are scored for meaning, grammar, and mechanics.

The Essay Composition subtest is scored for length, theme development, and organization. This subtest also is scored for spelling, capitalization, punctuation, and meaning. Scoring for correct/incorrect word sequences is valuable for capturing overall quality of the essay.

Answers to Questions About Written Language Tests

My child struggles with reading and writing. Her scores on the *WIAT-III* Reading Comprehension subtest were very low so I asked the team to assess her writing. The team declined, and said there was no need. What should I do?

If your child is a poor reader, she is likely to be a poor writer. When a child has poor reading skills, she should be assessed for written language difficulties. Both reading comprehension and written expression are based on oral language skills (e.g., vocabulary, syntax, and phonological awareness).

Write a letter to the school requesting a comprehensive evaluation of your daughter. Do not verbally request an evaluation. Include examples of your concerns about her reading and writing skills.

Request an evaluation of all areas related to her suspected disability, including written language and speech and language. You can use the sample letter to request an evaluation in Chapter 2, Evaluations by the School as a template.

A comprehensive school evaluation must include assessments of:

- Health

- Vision and hearing

- Social and emotional status

- General intelligence

- Academic performance

- Communication abilities

- Motor abilities

My daughter is failing several classes in high school. The quality of her writing is poor. When she was tested on the *Woodcock-Johnson III Tests of Achievement*, her Broad Written Language Composite score was in the average range. I'm confused.

The *WJ III* Broad Written Language Composite subtests only measure short written responses. These subtests do not measure your daughter's ability to write a story or an essay. The test, for the most part, did not measure her errors in grammar, spelling, or punctuation. Your child's teachers are unlikely to be as forgiving of grammar, spelling, and punctuation errors.

When evaluating your daughter's writing skills, the evaluator needs to test the skills that are actually required in school. Ask your evaluator about tests of written expression that measure the types of writing required in the classroom.

If your daughter has difficulty writing stories and essays, the evaluator should use a test that measures her skills in writing paragraphs, stories, and essays. Possible tests include:

- *Wechsler Individual Achievement Test, Third Edition*

- *Kaufman Test of Educational Achievement, Second Edition*

- *OWLS-II Written Expression Scale*

My son was tested on the *Test of Written Language, Third Edition (TOWL-3)* and later on the *Test of Written Language, Fourth Edition (TOWL-4)*. His scores on the *TOWL-4* indicated that his skills improved but we see no improvement in his writing. How can this be?

New editions of tests do not always measure the same sets of skills. The *TOWL-4* is substantially different from the *TOWL-3*. The picture prompts changed. The rules for scoring are different. Evaluators do not know to what degree the two editions of this test measure the same skills.

When measuring a child's progress, it is essential that you compare apples to apples and oranges to oranges. It is impossible to determine a child's progress by comparing scores on the *TOWL-3* and the *TOWL-4*.

In some cases, for the purpose of comparison, the evaluator may re-test the child with an out-of-date test. The evaluator should also administer a current test.

All About Tests and Assessments

My child's first grade teacher reports that he is having trouble learning to write. He scored in the average range on the *WJ III* Writing Samples subtest. An average score seems high to me, considering his difficulties.

Many tests of written expression are not sensitive to the skills required for first grade so they give inflated scores.

A written language assessment of a young child should measure indicators of early writing ability including handwriting quality, handwriting speed, spelling, and sentence writing.

On a spelling test, my child wrote neatly and scored in the average range. On a test that required him to write a story, his handwriting was messy and his spelling was poor. Does he need help with writing?

A child's handwriting skill varies depending on the task. The quality of handwriting is often related to how a child's memory is used by different skills.

When your child took the spelling test, he could focus on spelling and handwriting. When he wrote a story with sentences, he had to use his memory for many skills: vocabulary, sentence structure, organization, and planning.

The difference in his test scores suggests that he would benefit from direct instruction in handwriting.

He needs to learn to write longer assignments neatly. He may require assistive technology.

An occupational therapy assessment will clarify the nature of his writing problems and suggest solutions. You may also consider an assistive technology assessment. See Chapter 11, Assessments of Hearing, Visions, and Motor Skills.

My child has poor handwriting and was evaluated by an Occupational Therapist at school. The OT used the *Beery Buktenica Developmental Test of Visual-Motor Integration, Fifth Edition (VMI5)*. My child earned an average score. The OT said my child could write neatly if he tried harder. Is this correct? Does the *VMI5* test handwriting?

The *VMI5* measures the ability to copy geometric shapes and designs with pencil and paper. Handwriting is different. The letters of the alphabet are not just shapes.

When children write, they have to make links between their motor skills (how each letter is formed) and their language system (speech sounds in words). This is why some children are good at drawing but bad at handwriting. Handwriting is a special skill in its own right.

Some children cannot "write neater." Their problems are not about neatness. The quality of their handwriting depends on the task. Writing an essay requires more memory than writing words on a spelling test.

If legibility when writing a story or an essay is a problem, the school team should ensure that the child learns keyboarding skills and/or other forms of assistive technology.

My child's written work is full of spelling errors. I don't know if her problems are caused by a disability or lack of teaching. Can I request that the school evaluate her spelling?

Spelling is a component of written expression. Spelling should be included in a comprehensive evaluation of a child's writing difficulties.

Since you have concerns about your child's inability to spell, ask for a written language assessment. Provide the team with writing samples so team members can see how poor spelling affects the quality of her written work.

Tests that measure spelling skills include the *Test of Written Spelling, Fourth Edition*, the *WIAT-III*, the *KTEA-II*, and the *WJ III*. The evaluator may also use the *Words Their Way Spelling Inventory*.

Resources

Balsiger, L. (n.d.). *Assistive technology for writing*. Retrieved from www.bendlanguageandlearning.com/Assistive%20Technology%20for%20Writing.pdf

Berninger, V., & Wolf, B. (2012, March 14). *Understanding dysgraphia*. Retrieved from www.interdys.org/ewebeditpro5/upload/

Colorin, C. (2008). *Helping young children develop strong writing skills*. Retrieved from www.colorincolorado.org/article/21885/

Horowitz, S. (n.d.). *How to evaluate dysgraphia: FAQs*. Retrieved from www.ncld.org/types-learning-disabilities/dysgraphia/handwriting-ld-evaluations-faq-answers

Moats, L. (2011). *Understanding spelling*. Retrieved from www.interdys.org/ewebeditpro5/upload/SpellingRev.2011.pdf

Olinghouse, N. (2009, Summer). *Writing Assessment for Struggling Learners*. Retrieved from www.interdys.org/ewebeditpro5/upload/Writing_Assessment_Olinghouse

In Summation

Children with writing and spelling problems should be evaluated to identify underlying causes. There are tests that assess specific writing and spelling issues, and problems with penmanship. In this chapter, you learned about these tests.

In the next chapter, you will learn about problems related to learning mathematics and math assessments.

Endnotes

1. Farrall, M. (2013). The assessment of written syntax. *Perspectives on Language and Literacy.* 38(3), 31-36

2. Berninger, V. (1994). Directions for research on writing disabilities. In G. Lyon (Ed.), *Frames of reference for the assessment of learning disabilities* (pp. 419-439). Baltimore, MD: Brookes

3. National Council on Learning Disabilities. (n.d.). *What is dysgraphia?* Retrieved from www.ncld.org/types-learning-disabilities/dysgraphia/what-is-dysgraphia

4. Sterling, C., Farmer, M., Riddick, B., Morgan, S., & Matthews, C. (1998), *Adult dyslexic writing.* Dyslexia, 4: 1-15

5. Spear-Swerling, L. (2006). *The importance of teaching handwriting* Retrieved from www.readingrockets.org/article/27888/

Mathematics and Math Assessments

- Assessing Math Difficulties and Disabilities

- Mathematics Skills

- Tests of Mathematics

- Answers to Questions about Math Tests

- Assessing Math: Special Factors

Many children struggle with mathematics. If you are like most people, math was the most difficult and intimidating subject you faced in school. You may believe that if math doesn't come naturally, it will never be easy.

You may be tempted to overlook or dismiss your child's problems with math. Resist the desire to overlook your child's difficulties.

Math includes many skills and concepts. Your child may master some skills easily and struggle to learn others. For example, she may have trouble with multiplication, but have no difficulty learning geometry.

The goal of math in the early grades is to ensure that your child is proficient in whole numbers, fractions, decimals, and percentages. She needs to master these skills before she can learn algebra, geometry, and calculus.

When your child thinks with numbers, she will use different types of memory, language, attention, spatial reasoning, and higher-order thinking. She must learn basic math skills and concepts before she can solve advanced math problems.

You are your child's advocate. Your goal is to identify math problems early, before your child loses confidence and begins to fear math. Good jobs require basic math and computing skills. If your child's math skills are deficient, her options for the future will be limited. If you ensure that she masters math skills, you will improve her options for further education, employment, and independent living.

In this chapter, you will learn about math difficulties and disabilities and how math is assessed. You will learn about math skills, tests that are used to measure math skills, and answers to questions about math tests.

If your child has math difficulties or a math disability, he needs to receive explicit instruction in math computation and word problems. He also needs opportunities to practice math skills and receive feedback.[1]

Assessing Math Difficulties and Disabilities

Many children have difficulty learning or remembering arithmetic facts and carrying out basic numerical operations.

The school plans to evaluate my child for a math disability. What should a math assessment include?

A comprehensive math assessment should test your child's skills in math reasoning, math computation, and math fluency. A math evaluation may include:

- Basic number concepts

- Computation

- Measurement and estimation

- Telling time and money

- Word problems

- Fractions, decimals, and integers

- Fluency

- Higher-level math skills including algebra and geometry

A comprehensive math evaluation may also include:

- Language skills

- Cognitive abilities, including verbal reasoning

- Spatial thinking

- Memory and attention

- Processing speed

With a young child or an older child who has handwriting difficulty, the evaluator may assess number formation and the ability to write neatly in columns.

The evaluator should observe your child's behavior during testing. What items did she fail? [2] Did she have difficulty recalling or retrieving math facts or following multi-step directions? Did she add when she should subtract or transpose numbers? Did she use all the working space on the paper?[3]

The evaluator should describe the types of errors made and your child's response style. Did she use counting aids like finger counting or tally marks? Did she need to erase frequently?

If your child has a math disability, she is likely to feel anxiety at the thought of math.[4] The evaluator should describe signs of anxiety or distress in the evaluation report.

My daughter says she hates math. Math does not come easily to her but I think she can learn if she works at it. Should we get a math assessment?

A math assessment provides a sample of skills, not a complete inventory of everything your child knows.

When testing a young child, the examiner should supplement the norm-referenced test battery with criterion-referenced tests that can more thoroughly assess your child's mastery of number concepts and math facts.

When testing an older child, the same rule applies. If your child has difficulty with algebra, she is likely to have gaps in her knowledge of math facts, fractions, decimals, and integers (positive and negative numbers). A comprehensive assessment should identify these gaps and point the way to effective instruction.

Warning! Parents and teachers need to be aware that most tests of math do not assess higher-level skills in depth. For example, a test may not include problems that test your child's mastery of algebra and geometry.

My first grader is struggling to learn math. When can a child be evaluated to determine if he has a learning disability in math?

If your child is in first grade and is having difficulty learning basic facts, this may be an early sign of a math disability. If you have concerns about your child's ability to perform grade-level math tasks, have your child tested now.

Many children have math difficulties (MD). Fewer children have a math learning disability (MLD).

What is dyscalculia?

Dyscalculia is a specific learning disability in math reasoning and/or math calculation.[5] This term is often used in private sector evaluations and by researchers. The *Diagnostic and Statistical Manual of Mental Disorders* (*DSM-V*) refers to a math disability as a "specific learning disorder with impairment in mathematics."[6]

All About Tests and Assessments

What role does memory play in difficulties with math?

Good question! The term **active working memory** describes the ability to remember what you are doing while you are doing it. After your child completes one step of a problem, she will use that information to move on to the next step. Her active working memory allows her to hold the parts of the math problem in her head.

Assume your child needs to perform the mental computation 11 x 25. She may say, "10 times 25 is 250 and 1 times 25 is 25. If I add 25 to 250, I will have 275." She solved the problem by holding parts in her mind, then combining these parts for the answer.

Pattern recognition is another key part of math. Pattern recognition is the ability to identify broad themes and patterns in mathematics and transfer them into new situations. When your child is presented with a math word problem, she has to identify the pattern, and connect it to similar problems in her experience.

Memory for rules is essential in math. When your child is presented with a new problem, she must recall the rules for solving the problem from her long-term memory.[7]

Mathematics Skills

As you have learned, different tests measure different skills. Mathematics skills include:

Computational Skills: Young children perform basic math computational skills, including addition, subtraction, multiplication, and division. Older children work with fractions, positive and negative numbers, decimals, and percentages.

Math Reasoning: Your child may be asked to solve oral or written math word problems, interpret graphs, complete patterns, and estimate quantities.

Advanced Calculations: Your child may demonstrate skill with algebra, geometry, or calculus. Most tests measure a sample of advanced skills. The examiner should supplement tests of high-level math skills with criterion-referenced tests and work samples.

Practical Applications: Your child may be asked to tell time, work with money, or measure length, volume, and area.

Math Fluency: Your child may perform math computations while being timed.

Tests of Mathematics

You know that academic achievement tests include multiple-subject and single-subject tests. Multiple-subject tests that are often used to assess math include:

- *Kaufman Test of Educational Achievement, Second Edition (KTEA-II)*
- *Wechsler Individual Achievement Test, Third Edition (WIAT-III)*
- *Woodcock Johnson III Tests of Achievement (WJ III)*
- *Wechsler Intelligence Scale for Children, Fourth Edition (WISC-IV)*

Table 8-1 is a list of mathematics tests and subtests and the skills assessed by each test.

Table 8-1. Tests of Mathematics

Tests & Subtests	Computation	Math Reasoning	Advanced Calculations	Practical Applications	Fluency
Comprehensive Mathematical Abilities Test (CMAT)	√	√	√	√	
Kaufman Test of Educational Achievement, Second Edition (KTEA-II)	√	√	√	√	
KeyMath-3 Diagnostic Assessment (KeyMath-3)	√	√	√	√	
Test of Early Mathematics Ability, Third Edition (TEMA-3)	√	√			
Wechsler Individual Achievement Test, Third Edition (WIAT-III)	√	√	√	√	√
Wechsler Intelligence Scale for Children, Fourth Edition (WISC-IV)		√		√	
Woodcock-Johnson Tests of Achievement, Third Edition (WJ III ACH)	√	√	√	√	√

Kaufman Test of Educational Achievement, Second Edition (KTEA-II)

The *KTEA-II* includes two math subtests. The Math Computation subtest measures addition, subtraction, multiplication, division, fractions, decimals, integers, exponents, square roots, and algebra. The Math Concepts & Applications subtest focuses on number and operation concepts, time, money, measurement, geometry, interpreting data, and higher-level concepts. Scratch paper is permitted for higher-level items. A calculator is not allowed.

Wechsler Individual Achievement Test, Third Edition (WIAT-III)

The *WIAT-III* has several math subtests. The Math Problem Solving subtest measures basic concepts, money, measurement, time, graphs, word problems, geometry, and higher-level concepts. The Numerical Operations subtest measures basic concepts and operations, geometry, algebra, and calculus.

Math fluency is an important component of any math assessment. The Math Fluency subtest of the *WIAT-III* measures the number of correct calculations per minute for addition, subtraction, and multiplication.

Scratch paper is permitted. Calculators and pencils with erasers are not allowed.

Woodcock-Johnson Tests of Achievement, Third Edition (WJ III ACH)

The *WJ III* has three math subtests on the standard battery and one subtest on the extended battery. The Math Calculation subtest samples basic operations, trigonometric, logarithmic, and calculus operations. The Applied Problems subtest requires the child to make decisions about correct operations and perform basic calculations.

The Math Fluency subtest requires the child to perform addition, subtraction, and multiplication calculations while being timed. The supplemental subtest, Quantitative Concepts, measures basic math concepts and pattern recognition. A calculator is not allowed.

Wechsler Intelligence Scale for Children, Fourth Edition (WISC-IV)

The *WISC-IV* uses the Arithmetic subtest to assess math reasoning. The Arithmetic subtest measures the child's ability to solve orally presented word problems without using a pencil and paper. Although the Arithmetic subtest is part of an IQ test, it is a welcome addition to any math achievement battery.

Single-subject tests of math include:

- *KeyMath-3 Diagnostic Assessment (KeyMath-3)*

- *Comprehensive Mathematical Abilities Test (CMAT)*

KeyMath-3 Diagnostic Assessment (KeyMath-3)

The *KeyMath-3* is a norm-referenced test that includes subtests in three areas:

- **Basic Concepts:** Numeration, algebra, geometry, measurement, and data analysis

- **Operations:** Written and mental computational skills

- **Applications:** Problem-solving skills

The *KeyMath-3* can be administered to children between the ages of 4 ½ through 21. Although it may be used with high school students, the *KeyMath-3* does not measure higher-level math skills and may provide inflated scores for older students.

Comprehensive Mathematical Abilities Test (CMAT)

The *Comprehensive Mathematical Abilities Test (CMAT)* is designed to measure math reasoning, calculation, and applications. The *CMAT* attempts to measure math skills in ways that reflect how math is taught in schools. The *CMAT* provides composite scores in several areas:

- **Basic Calculations:** Addition, Subtraction, Multiplication, and Division.

- **Math Reasoning:** Math Problem Solving (word problems) and work with Charts, Tables, and Graphs.

- **Practical Applications:** Problem solving in the areas of Time, Money, and Measurement.

- **Advanced Calculations:** Algebra (solving for unknowns, polynomials, quadratics, and simultaneous linear equations), Geometry (area, volume, triangles, and circles), and Rational Numbers (fractions and decimals).

On the *CMAT*, the child is allowed to use a calculator on all subtests except those measuring computational skills. The evaluator must document the use of a calculator in the evaluation report.

The *CMAT* does ***not*** assess math fluency.

Answers to Questions about Math Tests

How is working memory assessed?

Working memory is a standard part of most cognitive batteries, including the *Wechsler Intelligence Scales,* the *Differential Ability Scales,* and the *Woodcock-Johnson III Tests of Cognitive Abilities.* Working memory can also be assessed with a test such as the *Working Memory Rating Scale* (*WMRS*).

These tests include subtests that assess different components of working memory. These subtests allow the evaluator to identify a child who has a poor working memory for his chronological age.

The evaluator may also use rating scales to identify a child who has a poor working memory. The *Working Memory Rating Scale* includes more than 20 descriptions of behavior ("She lost her place in a task with multiple steps" and "The child raised his hand but when called upon, he forgot his response"). The teacher rates how typical these behaviors are for the child. Rating scales are best used as one component of a comprehensive evaluation.

My child spends hours on math homework but he's failing math. His score on a math fluency subtest was way below average. Does he have a learning disability in math?

Your child is not fluent in math so he is failing. A comprehensive mathematics assessment will determine if he has a learning disability, and will document his strengths, areas of weakness, and his educational needs.

Children have different math difficulties and math disabilities.[8] Some have difficulty with the language of math. Others struggle with weaknesses in memory, retrieval, attention, processing speed, or spatial thinking.

Information from a comprehensive math assessment should be used to design a program of specialized math instruction and accommodations that is individualized to meet your child's needs.

One of my students is having difficulty learning fractions. Can we test for this problem?

Many children who struggle with math have visual-spatial weaknesses so they have difficulty thinking with shapes and designs. A child with visual-spatial weaknesses is likely to have problems in several areas, including:

- Number sense

- Understanding place value, decimals, and fractions

- Learning to tell time

- Interpreting graphs and charts

Typically, spatial thinking is measured on tests of cognitive skills, including the *Woodcock-Johnson Tests of Cognitive Abilities,* the *Wechsler Intelligence Scales,* and the *Differential Ability Scales, Second Edition.*

Another option is to assess the child's spatial thinking, visual-motor skills, and visual organization with the *Rey-Osterrieth Complex Figure Test (ROCF).*

On the *ROCF,* the child is asked to reproduce a complicated line drawing, first by copying it, then by drawing it from memory immediately or after a longer delay. The test requires the child to use different cognitive abilities, including visual-spatial abilities, attention, planning, and working memory. See Chapter 12 about Auditory, Visual, Visual Motor, and Sensory Processing Assessments.

My fourth grader struggles with arithmetic. Are there programs that help kids who are struggling in math?

Unfortunately, research about effective math programs is thin, especially when compared to research-based reading programs.

Before you look for a math program for your child, you need to have a clear sense of your child's strengths, weaknesses, and needs. The first step is to get a comprehensive assessment on your child. You can request that the school evaluate your child for a specific learning disability or you can get a psycho-educational evaluation from an evaluator in the private sector.

Research-Based Math Programs and Resources

Although curriculum publishers claim that their math programs are research-based, there is often little evidence to support these claims. The research on effective math programs is limited. When selecting a math intervention program, you need to identify the child's weaknesses and implement a program that targets these weaknesses.

My daughter is a poor reader. She is scheduled to take the *WIAT-III* Math Problem Solving subtest. Can the teacher read this test to her?

Yes. Most tests of math problem solving or math reasoning instruct the evaluator to read questions to the child. When questions are presented this way, the test is more likely to assess your daughter's math reasoning, not her reading comprehension.

Assessing Math: Special Factors

My daughter has high functioning autism and a learning disability in math. Can you recommend tests to measure her working memory and math skills?

Although your child has challenges that are unique to autism, her math evaluation should measure the same skills as an evaluation of a child who does not have autism.

Testing should identify the skills your child has mastered and the skills she needs to learn. Cognitive testing will provide information about skills that will help her learn math. Language testing may alert her teachers to difficulties in language usage and word meanings.

My 11 year old skips numbers and puts them in the wrong places. He doesn't seem to know whether to add or subtract or what the signs mean. Is this because he has ADHD? Should we have him tested for a math disability?

Many children with ADHD also have specific learning disabilities. Since your child has significant difficulty with math, he may have a learning disability in math calculation or math reasoning. Request that your child be evaluated.

My son is bright, talkative, and friendly but he is failing in math and English composition. The school plans to evaluate him. What do we need to know?

Your son needs a comprehensive evaluation that addresses *all areas* related to his suspected disability. Given his difficulties with math and written expression, the evaluator needs to test his cognitive abilities, including verbal comprehension, spatial

thinking, working memory, and processing speed. The evaluator should also test his oral language skills, and his achievement in reading, writing, and math.

Many children with weak math and writing skills also have weaknesses in spatial thinking, processing speed, and graphomotor skills so the evaluator should assess these areas.

My daughter is diagnosed with dyslexia. She enters middle school this year, but does not know her math facts. What should we do?

Children who have dyslexia often have weaknesses in math. Request that your daughter's math skills be assessed.

Resources

Krasa, N., Shunkwiler, S. (2009) *Number sense and number nonsense: Understanding the challenges of learning math.* Baltimore, MD: Paul H. Brookes Publishing Company

National Center for Learning Disabilities. *Ten helpful dyscalculia resources.* Retrieved from www.ncld.org/types-learning-disabilities/dyscalculia/helpful-math-resources

Khan Academy (www.khanacademy.org) is a free online collection of more than 4,000 math lessons. Khan Academy is used in many classrooms and can be accessed for direct instruction in math by students of any age.

In Summation

In this chapter, you learned about math skills, math difficulties, and learning disabilities in math. You learned about math tests and the skills these tests measure.

In the next chapter, you will learn about Speech and Language Assessments.

Endnotes

1. www2.ed.gov/about/bdscomm/list/mathpanel/index.html. www2.ed.gov/about/bdscomm/list/mathpanel/report/instructional-practices.pdf

2. Willis, J.O., & Dumont, R.P. (2002). *Guide to identification of learning disabilities* (3rd ed.). Peterborough, NH: Author

3. Sattler, J.M. (2008). *Assessment of children: Cognitive foundations* (5th Ed.) San Diego CA: Author

4. Maloney, E.A., & Beilock, S.L. (2012). *Math anxiety: Who has it, why it develops and how to guard against it.* Retrieved from: www.ncbi.nlm.nih.gov/pubmed/22784928

5. Butterworth, B., & Reigosa Crespo, V. (2007). Information processing deficits in dyscalculia. In D. Berch & M. Mazzocco (EDs.), *Why is math so hard for some children? The nature and origins of mathematical learning difficulties and disabilities (pp.65-81).* Baltimore, MD: Paul H. Brookes Publishing

6. American Psychiatric Association (2013). *Diagnostic and statistical manual of mental disorders,* (5th ed). Arlington, VA: American Psychiatric Association, p. 67

7. Public Broadcasting Service. (n.d.). *Misunderstood minds: Basics of mathematics.* Retrieved from www.pbs.org/wgbh/misunderstoodminds/mathbasics.html

8. Mazzocco, M.M. (2007). Defining and differentiating mathematical learning disabilities and difficulties. In D. Berch & M. Mazzocco (Eds.), *Why is math so hard for some children? The nature and origins of mathematical learning difficulties and disabilities (pp.29-47).* Baltimore, MD: Paul H. Brookes Publishing

9 Speech and Language Assessments

- Assessing Speech and Language Problems

- Speech and Language Skills

- Tests of Receptive and Expressive Language

- Vocabulary Tests

- Speech and Articulation Tests

- Apraxia Tests

- Pragmatics and Social Language Evaluations

- Answers to Questions about Speech and Language Assessments

As your child advances through school, he will use language to communicate, ask questions, and express his thoughts. If he has speech or language difficulties, you need to ensure that his problems are correctly identified and he receives the therapy he needs.

If your child has a speech disorder, he may have difficulty with articulation (speech), fluency (ease and accuracy), or voice (pitch and harmonics). If he has an expressive language disorder, he is likely to struggle when expressing his thoughts, ideas, and feelings. If he has a receptive language disorder, he will have difficulty listening, remembering, and understanding others.

All About Tests and Assessments

If your child has a social pragmatic language disorder, he will have difficulty with nonverbal types of communication including personal space and body language. He may not understand figurative language.

In this chapter, you will learn about tests and assessments for speech and language disorders. Speech and language disorders and speech impairments often have an adverse impact on the child's educational performance. "Speech language impairment" is a disability category in the Individuals with Disabilities Education Act.[1]

Assessing Speech and Language Problems

My child has speech and language problems. Friends and family often cannot understand what he says. What do I need to know about speech and language assessments?

A comprehensive speech and language assessment will assess your child's receptive and expressive language skills. The assessment should include:

- Background and medical history, language developmental milestones

- Information from teachers and service providers

- Interviews of family and child

- Observations of child

- Audiometric hearing screening

- Review of the child's hearing, visual, motor, and cognitive status

- Tests of speech, spoken and non-spoken language, and communication

- Recommendations[2]

Who administers speech and language evaluations?

Speech and language pathologists (SLPs) conduct speech and language (S/L) evaluations. The SLP may request that your child's hearing and vision be tested.

Neuropsychologists, school psychologists, and learning disabilities specialists may assess a child's language skills. For additional information about sensory impairments, including hearing and vision problems, see Chapter 11, Assessments of Hearing, Vision, and Motor Skills.

My four-year old child's speech is delayed. How can I tell if he has a language problem or is just a "late-bloomer"?

Speech language problems will affect your child's social skills, behavior, and academic skills. If these problems are not identified and treated early, they will continue or get worse. Early speech and language intervention helps with reading, writing, and social relationships.

If you suspect that your child has a speech language delay, trust your instincts. Refer your child to your school district for an evaluation. If your school district offers to do a screening, you may decline the screening and ask for a comprehensive speech language evaluation by an SLP.

After a SLP assesses your child's language and analyzes his speech, she will advise you about the steps you should take. She may suggest ways you can stimulate your child's language, or she may refer your child to an early intervention program.[3]

Table 9-1 is a brief overview of developmental milestones in language. If your child is delayed in meeting his milestones, you need to consult with a speech and language professional.

Oral Expression (Oral Ex): Child responds verbally to prompts and directions and expresses his thoughts with grammar and logic.

Vocabulary (Vocab): Child demonstrates understanding of word meanings, labels pictures, and provides words with the same meaning.

Syntax: Child uses words in specific order to form sentences, combines facts into sentences, and repeats sentences from memory.

Table 9-1. Developmental Milestones in Language

Stage	Developmental Milestones
Before birth	Hearing develops at 26 weeks.
Infancy	Seeks out smiling faces and eye contact; begins to coo and babble.
12 Months	Utters single words to express needs and wants.
18 to 24 Months	Uses two word phrases to express wants and control the behavior of others.
Ages 2 to 5	Vocabulary increases dramatically. Speaks in longer phrases, learns how to ask questions.
School-Age Child	Expresses needs, wants, and feelings. Realizes that words have sounds. Speaks about past, present, and future. Uses language to hint and to joke.

Speech and Language Skills

Speech and language skills include:

Listening: Child responds to questions or points to pictures based on directions or passages that are read aloud.

Semantics: Child demonstrates understanding of word meanings.

Nonliteral and Abstract Language (Nonlit/Abstract): Child explains the meaning of figurative expressions and idioms, makes inferences, and interprets words with multiple meanings.

Speech Articulation (Artic): Child makes the speech sounds that are part of his dialect or language.

The child may also be required to perform tasks related to memory, sound discrimination, phonological awareness, and pragmatics (social language).

No test of language assesses all areas and skills. Different tests measure different skills. Table 9-2 lists tests that measure aspects of oral language.

Tests of Receptive and Expressive Language

The evaluator should always assess the child's receptive and expressive language skills. If your child has a receptive language disorder, he may:

- Misunderstand what people say

- Have trouble following spoken directions

- Have difficulty organizing his thoughts

A receptive language disorder is also called a language processing disorder. Some children with receptive language disorders have auditory processing disorders. Many children with language processing disorders may appear to have attention deficits.

How will the evaluator assess my child's receptive language skills?

A receptive language assessment may include tests of your child's vocabulary, grammar and syntax, ability to follow directions, and listening.

Tests of receptive language allow your child to show what he knows without having to speak. On some receptive language tests, your child points to pictures and performs tasks in response to directions. For example, on the *Oral and Written Language Scales, Second Edition (OWLS-II)*, the child points to the picture that best illustrates spoken words.

On the *Clinical Evaluation of Language Fundamentals, Fifth Edition (CELF-5)*, the child is asked to follow directions and point to objects. He may point to pictures that illustrate spoken words and sentences. He may also select words that go together, select correct responses to a target question, and answer questions based on paragraphs that are read to him.

If your child has an expressive language disorder, he may:

- Understand more than he can say

- Have difficulty putting words together in sentences

- Use tenses (past, present, future) improperly

- Have trouble finding words and organizing his thoughts

- Struggle in conversations and classroom discussions

- Have difficulty with writing

Table 9-2. Tests that Measure Speech and Language Skills (continued on next page)

Speech and Language Tests	Listening	Oral Ex	Vocab	Syntax	Nonlit/ Abstract	Speech Artic	Other
Clinical Evaluation of Language Fundamentals, Fifth Edition (CELF-5)	√		√	√			√
Comprehensive Assessment of Spoken Language (CASL)	√		√	√	√		√
Comprehensive Receptive and Expressive Vocabulary Test, Third Edition (CREVT-3)			√				
Diagnostic Evaluation of Articulation and Phonology (DEAP)						√	
Goldman-Fristoe Test of Articulation, Second Edition (GFTA-2)						√	
Expressive One-Word Picture Vocabulary Test, Fourth Edition (EOWPVT-4)			√				
Expressive Vocabulary Test, Second Edition (EVT-2)			√				
Illinois Test of Psycholinguistic Abilities, Third Edition (ITPA-3)			√	√			√
Kaufman Speech Praxis Test for Children (KSPT)						√	
Khan-Lewis Phonological Analysis, Second Edition (KLPA-2)						√	
Oral and Written Language Scales, Second Edition (OWLS-II)	√	√					
Peabody Picture Vocabulary Test, Fifth Edition (PPVT-5)			√				
Preschool Language Scale, Fifth Edition (PLS-5)	√	√					
Receptive One-Word Picture Vocabulary Test, Fourth Edition (ROWPVT-4)			√				

All About Tests and Assessments

Table 9-2. Tests that Measure Speech and Language Skills (continued from previous page)

Speech and Language Tests	Listening	Oral Ex	Vocab	Syntax	Nonlit/ Abstract	Speech Artic	Other
Stuttering Prediction Instrument for Young Children (SPI)							√
Stuttering Severity Instruction, Fourth Edition (SSI-4)							√
Test of Adolescent and Adult Language, Fourth Edition (TOAL-4)			√	√			
Test of Auditory Processing Skills, Third Edition (TAPS-3)	√			√			√
Test of Language Development, Primary – Fourth Edition (TOLD: P-4)			√	√	√		√
Test of Language Development, Intermediate – Fourth Edition (TOLD: I-4)			√	√			
Test of Pragmatic Language, Second Edition (TOPL-2)							√

If your child cannot express himself, he is likely to get frustrated and behave inappropriately. Parents and teachers often focus on controlling behavior. If adults do not address the communication and expressive language problems that are causing the child's frustration, his behavior problems are likely to escalate. See Chapter 13, Adaptive and Functional Behavior Assessments.

How will the evaluator assess my child's expressive language skills?

The evaluator will assess your child's expressive language skills with tests that require him to speak. The tests selected will vary depending on your child's age and areas of concern.

On the *Clinical Evaluation of Language Fundamentals, Fifth Edition (CELF-5)*, your child may repeat orally presented sentences, use specific words or phrases to create sentences about pictures, or produce meaningful and grammatical sentences using words presented visually and orally.

On the *Comprehensive Assessment of Spoken Language (CASL)*, the examiner may ask your child to provide antonyms (opposite words), fix sentences that contain incorrect grammar, or change the meaning of words.

My child has difficulty expressing his thoughts. His scores were in the average range on the Oral Expression subtest of the *Wechsler Individual Achievement Test, Third Edition (WIAT-III)*. The school says he doesn't need help. I do not agree.

Your question is a good example of why a team should never use results of one test or subtest to make educational decisions. The Oral Expression subtest in the *Wechsler Individual Achievement Test, Third Edition (WIAT-III)* is not designed to identify all children with expressive language difficulties or disabilities. It is not typically administered by an SLP.

The Oral Expression subtest in the *Wechsler Individual Achievement Test, Third Edition (WIAT-III)* includes three components:

• Expressive Vocabulary

• Oral Word Fluency

• Sentence Repetition

The *Expressive Vocabulary* section requires the child to provide words in response to pictures and orally-presented definitions. The *Oral Word Fluency* section requires the child to name objects in a given category while

being timed. The *Sentence Repetition* section requires the child to listen to a sentence, and then repeat it verbatim.

The *Oral Expression* subtest is not a substitute for a speech and language evaluation that assesses your child in all areas related to his suspected speech and language disability.

If your child is having difficulties with language, request a comprehensive speech and language evaluation from the school, or arrange for an evaluation by a speech and language pathologist in the private sector.

Vocabulary Tests

Some vocabulary tests measure receptive skills, i.e., the understanding of word meanings. Other vocabulary tests measure expressive skills, the ability to name a picture or an object, or provide a synonym to an orally presented word.

When my daughter speaks, she often has to stop to "find" the next word. How can this problem be assessed?

Word retrieval or word finding are terms that describe your child's ability to access words from her memory. If there is a significant difference between your child's performance on tests of receptive and expressive language, she may have deficits in word finding or word retrieval.

Vocabulary tests that are used to make this comparison include:

• *The Peabody Picture Vocabulary Test, Fifth Edition (PPVT-5)* and the *Expressive Vocabulary Test, Second Edition (EVT-2)*

All About Tests and Assessments

- The *Receptive One-Word Picture Vocabulary Test, Fourth Edition (ROWPVT-4)* and the *Expressive One-Word Picture Vocabulary Test, Fourth Edition (EOWPVT-4)*

- The *Comprehensive Receptive and Expressive Vocabulary Test, Third Edition (CREVT-3)*

There are different types of word finding difficulties so word finding or word retrieval should be assessed as part of a comprehensive speech and language evaluation.[4]

On the *Peabody Picture Vocabulary Test, Fifth Edition (PPVT-5)*, my child earned a very high score when asked to point to pictures of words. On the *Expressive Vocabulary Test, Second Edition (EVT-2)*, he earned a very low score when asked to name pictures and provide synonyms. Which score should we rely on?

Different vocabulary tests assess skills differently, but each test provides useful information about your child's skills and difficulties. The fact that your child's scores on these tests are significantly different is important. The scores suggest that he has word retrieval problems.

The *PPVT-5* measures your child's understanding of word meanings - his receptive vocabulary. The *EVT-2* measures his ability to name pictures or provide synonyms to spoken words - his expressive vocabulary.

A child who has difficulties with word retrieval may say, "I know it, but I can't remember it" or "The word is on the tip of my tongue."

When a child has word retrieval problems, it is hard to take tests, talk in class, write, calculate math problems, and socialize with others. Word retrieval problems are frustrating!

Speech and Articulation Tests

My first grader's speech is soft and difficult to understand. Is he too young to be tested?

No. If your child's speech is not clear or people cannot understand him, he needs to be evaluated. Do not delay.

If you have concerns about your child's speech, be proactive. Get advice from speech and language professionals. Early intervention is highly effective.

What should an evaluation of articulation and phonological disorders include?

A speech and language assessment should describe your child's ability to articulate sounds with accuracy.[5] The evaluation should include tests that identify articulation errors. Tests of articulation include the *Goldman-Fristoe Test of Articulation, Second Edition (GFTA-2)* and the *Diagnostic Evaluation of Articulation and Phonology (DEAP)*.

An evaluation should also include speech samples and an analysis of the sounds your child can produce with modeling and prompting. The SLP may recommend speech therapy, or monitor changes over time.

A speech evaluation should identify factors that contribute to the speech disorder. Some speech problems are the result of physical factors - hearing loss, cleft lip or palate, cerebral palsy, dysarthria, and acquired apraxia. In other cases, no physical cause is identified.

My child stutters. His classmates tease him. His teacher says he will grow out of it. How long do we have to wait?

Do not wait. Your child who stutters has disruptions in speech flow that cause him to repeat words or parts of words: "D-d-d-don't go." He may prolong sounds: "Sssssam fell down." He works hard to rearrange his words so he can pronounce them smoothly. He may also use filler words such as "um," "you know," or "like."

You need to get a comprehensive speech and language evaluation by a SLP now.

The evaluation will include observations, tests, and interviews.[6] The SLP will ask if there is a family history of stuttering. She will observe your child in different settings and document stuttering behaviors and language skill. She will observe your child's behavior. Is he stressed or embarrassed?

The pathologist will also assess your child's risk for long-term problems. If needed, she will work with you to develop a treatment plan or an IEP. Many children who stutter qualify for stuttering therapy because their speech places them at risk for teasing.

Apraxia Tests

My child's speech is choppy and hard to understand. He understands language better than he can speak. His doctor thinks he may have childhood apraxia of speech. What is apraxia of speech? Should he have a speech and language evaluation?

Childhood apraxia of speech (CAS) is a motor speech disorder. If your child has CAS, he has problems saying sounds, syllables, and words. He knows what he wants to say but his brain has difficulty coordinating his muscles to make sounds, syllables, and words.

Yes, your child needs to be evaluated by a SLP who has expertise in CAS. All children with CAS do not have the same symptoms or needs. In addition, an audiologist should evaluate your child's hearing to make sure hearing problems are not contributing to your child's speech difficulties.

What tests should be included in an evaluation for childhood apraxia of speech?

In an evaluation for childhood apraxia of speech (CAS), the speech language pathologist should focus on three areas:

- Oral motor skills

- Pitch and intonation when speaking

- Pronunciation of speech sounds in isolation and in context[7]

Testing oral-motor skills may include:

- Checking for signs of weakness or low muscle tone in the lips, jaw, and tongue

- Having the child move his tongue, smile, and frown to see how he coordinates the movement of his mouth

- Evaluating the coordination and sequencing of muscle movements for speech

Pitch and intonation are tested by:

- Listening to the child to make sure that he appropriately stresses syllables in words and words in sentences

- Determining if the child uses pitch and pauses to mark different types of sentences (e.g., questions vs. statements) and different portions of a sentence

Testing pronunciation of speech sounds may include:

- Evaluating your child's ability to make vowel and consonant sounds

- Testing his ability to say individual sounds and sound combinations

- Determining if others understand your child when he uses words, phrases, and conversational speech

The SLP may also examine your child's receptive and expressive language skills and his literacy skills to determine if he has problems in these areas.[8]

Pragmatics and Social Language Evaluations

My child has autism. The evaluator said he has weaknesses in pragmatics. What are pragmatics?

Pragmatics is a term for the rules of social language. These rules govern how people use language and how they interact socially. Raising your hand before speaking in class and knowing when and how to take turns are examples of pragmatics. Pragmatics also includes making eye contact and maintaining appropriate personal space and body orientation.

Pragmatics includes three communication skills:

- Using language for different purposes

- Changing language according to the needs of the listener or situation

- Following rules for conversations and storytelling[9]

If your child is on the autism spectrum or has a nonverbal learning disability, he may not know how to use language appropriately in social situations. Expect him to make inappropriate or irrelevant comments.

Although your child has a communication disorder, he may appear rude or disrespectful. Adults may view this as a behavior problem.

How are pragmatics evaluated?

The evaluator often tests pragmatics with "what would you do?" questions.

On the *Test of Pragmatic Language, Second Edition (TOPL-2),* and the *Comprehensive Assessment of Spoken Language (CASL)* Pragmatics subtest, the evaluator asks the child to describe how he makes introductions, requests help, hints, and adjusts his communication style in different settings.

Sadly, there is often a difference between answering a "what would you do?" question correctly, and actually responding correctly in the social situation. An assessment of pragmatics should include informal observations of the child in different environments - in school, at home, and in the community. Rating systems can be used to document how your child uses language skills to interact socially.[10]

Answers to Questions about Speech and Language Assessments

The school is evaluating my three-year-old for autism. His ability to communicate is limited. The evaluation will include a speech and language assessment. What should we expect from this assessment?

Communication and social skills problems are often early symptoms of autism. A SLP is an essential member of your child's diagnostic and treatment team. She should be involved early in the evaluation process. She will use tests, checklists, and observations to assess your child's communication skills and his progress over time.

My child's teacher says his language usage is "concrete." What does this mean?

If your child's language is concrete, he uses language literally. He understands messages that are clearly and directly stated. He may not draw conclusions or think inferentially.

When a child has a concrete understanding of the world, he often begins to have difficulties around third grade. He may not get jokes or commonly used expressions such as, "It's raining cats and dogs." As he progresses through school, he may struggle with language arts, social studies, and science.

All language tests do not measure abstract language skills. The *Comprehensive Assessment of Spoken Language (CASL)* measures aspects of abstract language. Language tests or cognitive tests that have the child categorize words or identify what words or concepts have in common are useful when assessing a child whose language is concrete.

If your child uses language literally, he will need direct, systematic instruction in the higher-level language skills. These skills will improve his relationships with other children, and will help him participate in class.

My daughter has a nonverbal learning disability and often misunderstands what people say. After the school tested her with the *Clinical Evaluation of Language Fundamentals, Fifth Edition (CELF-5),* they said she does not qualify for speech services. I don't get it.

Your question is another example of why educational decisions should never be based on one test or subtest. If the team only tested your daughter with the *CELF-5*, they did not do the comprehensive evaluation that is required before deciding if your child is eligible for special education services.

To assess your child's pragmatics, an evaluator should use tests that are designed to assess pragmatics. The core subtests of the *CELF-5* do not measure pragmatics although the *CELF-5* does have a *Pragmatics Profile* that examines a child's use of language. The evaluation should have assessed your child's conversational skills, ability to use language strategically, and nonverbal communication.

If you disagree with the school's evaluation, you have a right to request an Independent Educational Evaluation (IEE). Or you can get a comprehensive speech and language evaluation by a speech and language pathologist in the private sector.

The evaluation should assess your child's conversational skills, ability to use language strategically, and nonverbal communication. Present this new evaluation with the examiner's recommendations to your child's school team. Although the school is not required to accept the examiner's findings and recommendations. they are required to "consider" any new evaluation. See Chapter 2 for a discussion of what the law requires.

In Summation

In this chapter, you learned about assessments of speech and language skills. You learned about developmental milestones in language, language skills, and common speech and language disorders. You also learned the importance of pragmatics and social communication.

In the next chapter, we'll explore evaluations for specific learning disabilities and Attention-Deficit/Hyperactivity Disorder (ADHD).

Resources

American Speech-Language-Hearing Association. (n.d.) *Directory of Speech-Language Pathology Assessment Instruments*. Retrieved from www.asha.org/assessments.aspx

American Speech-Language-Hearing Association. (n.d.). *Books about Communication*. Retrieved from www.asha.org/public/books.htm

Endnotes

1. 20 U.S.C. §1401(3); 34 C.F.R. §300.8(c)(11)

2. American Speech-Language-Hearing Association. (n.d.). *Assessment and evaluation of speech-language disorders in schools*. Retrieved from: www.asha.

org/SLP/Assessment-and-Evaluation-of-
Speech-Language-Disorders-in-Schools

3. American-Speech-Language-Hearing
Association. (n.d.) *Late blooming
or language problem?* Retrieved
from: www.asha.org/public/speech/
disorders/LateBlooming.htm

4. *German, D. (2009, February 10). Child
word finding: Student voices enlighten us.
The ASHA Leader.* Retrieved from: www.
asha.org/Publications/leader/2009/090210/
f090210a.htm

5. Hulit, L., Howard, M., Fahey, K. (2010).
*Born to talk: An introduction to speech and
language development.* Upper Saddle River,
New Jersey: Pearson

6. American Speech-Language-Hearing
Association. (n.d.). *Stuttering.* Retrieved
from: www.asha.org/public/speech/
disorders/stuttering.htm

7. American Speech-Language-Hearing
Association. (n.d.). *Childhood apraxia
of speech.* Retrieved from: www.
asha.org/public/speech/disorders/
ChildhoodApraxia.htm

8. Ibid.

9. American Speech-Language-Hearing
Association. (n.d.). *Social use (pragmatics).*
Retrieved from: www.asha.org/public/
speech/development/Pragmatics.htm

10. Paul, R. (n.d.). *Social skills development,
assessment, and programming in school-
aged speakers with autism spectrum
disorders.* Retrieved from: http://medicine.
yale.edu/childstudy/autism/ldcd/
presentations/80268_social_skills.pdf

10 Evaluations for Learning Disabilities and Attention-Deficit/Hyperactivity Disorders (ADHD)

- Assessing Specific Learning Disabilities

- Assessing Attention-Deficit/ Hyperactivity Disorders (ADHD)

- Assessing Executive Functioning Skills

- Legal Requirements for Identifying Specific Learning Disabilities

- Response to Intervention (RTI)

In this chapter, you will learn about assessments for specific learning disabilities and Attention-Deficit/Hyperactivity Disorders (ADHD). You will learn about changes to the law about special education eligibility for children with specific learning disabilities and the role of Response to Intervention (RTI) in identifying children who may have specific learning disabilities.

Learning disabilities are neurobiological conditions. Learning disabilities are not caused by environmental factors, poverty, or cultural differences. Learning disabilities often co-exist with other neurological conditions like Attention-Deficit/ Hyperactivity Disorder (ADHD), mood

disorders, and anxiety disorders. The terms learning disability and specific learning disability are used interchangeably.

Assessing Specific Learning Disabilities

If your child has a specific learning disability, his disability affects *specific* areas. For example, math may be a strength for your child, although he struggles with reading and written language. He may have trouble listening or speaking. Or he may have learning disabilities that affect several areas – reading, written language, spelling, and math.

Your child's learning disability may be identified because there is a severe discrepancy between his ability to learn and his actual academic performance. If his team determines that he has a disability and needs specialized instruction, he may be eligible for special education services and an Individualized Education Program (IEP).

My son is bright but has always struggled to learn in school. In most subjects, his grades are poor. Should I have him evaluated for a learning disability?

The only way to know if your child has a learning disability is to get a comprehensive psycho-educational evaluation. A comprehensive evaluation will answer your questions about whether your child is performing at grade level *and* at his intelligence level in reading, spelling, writing, and math.

Depending on the test results, the evaluator may do additional testing. At a minimum, the evaluation should include:

- Intelligence tests
- Academic achievement tests
- Auditory processing tests
- Tests of visual perceptual processing skills

What should be included in an evaluation for a specific learning disability?

An evaluation for a specific learning disability should assess your child's intellectual ability and academic skills. The evaluation should include:

- Background and family history
- Interviews with parents, teachers, and the child, if appropriate
- Intelligence (IQ) testing
- Academic achievement testing
- Additional testing, depending on child's presenting problem and test findings
- Classroom observations

Intelligence tests measure your child's ability to learn, memory, phonological processing, processing speed, and other skills. Academic achievement tests measure his listening, speaking, reading, writing, and math skills. See Chapters 5-8 about academic achievement tests.

An evaluation for a specific learning disability should assess your child's skills in reading, including:

- Phonological awareness

- Knowledge of speech sounds, including vowels, consonants, blends

- Reading comprehension

- Silent reading

- Oral reading

An evaluation may include informal tests and criterion-referenced tests that assess your child's written and oral expression, and listening comprehension. The evaluation should include observations of your child's behavior and classroom work samples.[1]

The evaluation should address all areas related to your child's suspected disability. A comprehensive psycho-educational evaluation will give you a roadmap for the future and will help you track your child's progress over time.

How can I prepare for my child's evaluation?

Prepare to answer questions about your child's early development, health, and experiences at home and in school. The examiner may ask about your observations of your child's behavior at home and in the neighborhood. She may ask you and your child's teacher to complete questionnaires about your child's behavior.

If you are providing your child with extra help with homework, reviewing material,

and studying for tests, or if you arranged for your child to receive tutoring, be sure to let the evaluator know about these learning supports.

What information is included in the evaluation report?

The evaluation report should describe test conditions, how your child responded to the test situation, and your child's behavior during testing.

The report should include a list of tests given and your child's scores as standard scores, percentile ranks, and age and grade equivalent scores. These scores document how your child performed when compared to his peers.

The report should also include recommendations for your child's educational program and suggestions for accommodations and modifications.

When I met with the school team, they said they had to do a classroom observation. Is this right?

Yes, if your child is being evaluated for a specific learning disability, a classroom observation is a required part of the evaluation.

An observation documents your child's academic performance and behavior in his areas of difficulty.[2] The school *must* observe your child in the classroom. If your child is not in school, the observation must be conducted in an age-appropriate setting.[3]

Who is qualified to diagnose specific learning disabilities?

After school professionals evaluate your child, the school team may *identify* your child with a learning disability. All team members—including parents—provide input to this decision.

A comprehensive assessment to *diagnose* a specific learning disorder is conducted by professionals who have expertise in psychological/cognitive assessment and specific learning disorders.[4]

A psychologist evaluated my child and diagnosed him with dyslexia. The school team said dyslexia is not a qualifying disability so they will not provide services. What should I do?

The team is misinformed. Dyslexia is a specific learning disability, and is listed in the legal definition of "specific learning disability" in the Individuals with Disabilities Education Act and federal special education regulations.[5]

When determining if your child has a disability and needs special education services, the team must consider other evaluations and information provided by you. The team may accept the psychologist's evaluation and diagnosis and use it to determine if your child is eligible for special education services. Or the team may decide to do additional testing.[6]

Parents are often surprised to learn that a medical or psychiatric diagnosis is not sufficient for a child to be eligible for special education and related services.

In determining special education eligibility, a school team that includes the child's parents must "identify" your child with a qualifying disability and must decide if your child *needs* specialized instruction.

The school evaluations show that my child has a learning disability. What can I do to help my child learn and catch up?

Educate yourself. If your child is like most children with learning disabilities, schoolwork and homework is hard. Your child may have teachers who believe your child is lazy, unmotivated, and just needs to "try harder."

Going to school and learning is your child's job. If he has difficulty learning, he is likely to feel frustrated, helpless, and hopeless. He needs to know that he can learn, but he needs to be taught by teachers who have specialized training. Many children with learning disabilities go on to college.

Assessing Attention-Deficit/ Hyperactivity Disorders (ADHD)

Attention-Deficit/Hyperactivity Disorders (ADHD) are neurological conditions that can occur alone, or with other learning disabilities.

Two federal laws protect the rights of eligible children with ADHD—the Individuals with Disabilities Education Act (IDEA) and Section 504 of the Rehabilitation Act of 1973 (Section 504). The regulations that implement these laws require school districts to provide a "free appropriate public education" to all children who meet the eligibility criteria in these laws.

My child has ADHD. He is very active and has difficulty staying on a task. Can he be tested?

Of course. Most children with ADHD test very well. An evaluation is highly structured. Directions are administered one step at a time.

Although some children with ADHD are distractible, impulsive, or hyperactive, a child's behavior during testing is often different from his behavior in the classroom. The assessment provides a window into how your child functions within a highly structured, one-on-one situation, without the distractions in a classroom.

My daughter has ADHD. Our doctor advised us to request special education from her school. The school said she is not eligible for special education because she makes passing grades. Now what?

In *Wrightslaw: All About Tests and Assessments*, you have learned that children must meet two criteria to be eligible for special education services. If your daughter is diagnosed with ADHD and *by reason thereof, needs special education and related services,* she should be eligible for special education under one of three disability categories in the IDEA.

- Other Health Impairment (OHI)
- Specific Learning Disability (SLD)
- Emotional Disturbance[7]

Can a child with a disability who receives passing grades and is passing from grade to grade be eligible for special education?

Yes. School personnel often advise parents that their children are not eligible for special education because they make passing grades and are passing from grade to grade. This is not correct.

The law requires schools to provide a free, appropriate education to any child with a disability who needs special education "even though the child has not failed or been retained in a course or grade, and is advancing from grade to grade."[8]

If your child has a disability but does not need special education services, he may be eligible for protections under Section 504 of the Rehabilitation Act. If ADHD adversely affects his ability to learn—a major life activity for children—she may qualify for services under Section 504.[9]

My child has ADHD. His teachers say he is smart but his scores on the IQ test are low. What happened?

When a child has ADHD, many things compete for his attention. His body may be in constant motion. If he is distractible, his ability to pay attention to tasks will vary. Tests may not measure his true ability to learn.

All About Tests and Assessments

The evaluator is responsible for determining if your child's test scores accurately represent his abilities, or if they are measure his behaviors and the impact of his disability.

My son has so much energy, he is constantly fidgeting and out of his seat in class. He has a short attention span and a poor memory. Could he have ADHD?

The only way to know if your child has ADHD is to have him undergo a thorough evaluation. A comprehensive evaluation for ADHD includes several components:

- Background and family history

- Interviews with parents and teachers

- Psycho-education evaluation to assess intelligence and academic skills

- Responses to standardized behavior rating scales

If your child has problems with auditory memory, speech, or reading, these may be symptoms of an auditory processing disorder. If your child seems to hear sounds, but does not appear to process what is said, her assessment should include an auditory processing assessment.

The evaluation may include neuropsychological tests to assess your child's memory, executive functioning (planning, organizing and motivation), visual-spatial processing, visual-motor skills, auditory processing, and speed of processing.

The evaluator will look for symptoms of inattentiveness, hyperactivity, and impulsivity that are apparent before age 12.[10] These symptoms must occur in two or more settings.

Assessing Executive Functioning Skills

What are executive functioning skills?

Executive functioning skills fall into two broad areas: planning/organizing and regulating behavior.[11] Executive functioning skills allow your child to:

- Pay attention and remember details

- Plan ahead and manage time

- Think about different ways to solve problems

- Keep track of more than one thing at once

- Compare, contrast, and organize new information

- Evaluate ideas and reflect on his work

- Get organized and stay organized

- Wait to speak until called upon[12]

If your child has a learning disability, attention deficit disorder, or a developmental disability, he is likely to have weaknesses in executive functioning skills.

What tests are used to measure executive functioning skills?

Executive functioning skills should be assessed as part of a comprehensive evaluation. Cognitive tests, including the *Wechsler Intelligence Scales*, measure working memory and processing speed. Questionnaires and rating scales ask teachers and parents about the child's behavior at home and in school.

A clinical psychologist diagnosed my child with an executive functioning disorder. The school team says he is not eligible for special education. Is this true?

The term "executive functioning" describes skills. Executive functioning is not a disability. A child with executive functioning deficits may be eligible for special education if he has a qualifying disability – possibly a specific learning disability or other health impairment.

A child must meet two criteria to be eligible for special education services and an IEP. He must have a qualifying disability, and because of the disability, he must **need** special education services.

Response to Intervention (RTI)

The process of determining if a child responds to scientific, research-based intervention is called Response to Intervention (RTI). RTI includes universal screening and high-quality instruction in the general education classroom for all students, including struggling learners and children with disabilities.

The purpose of RTI is to identify children who have difficulty learning early, and to

---

Legal Requirements for Identifying Specific Learning Disabilities

When Congress reauthorized the Individuals with Disabilities Education Act in 2004, they changed the requirements for determining if a child has a learning disability and is eligible for special education services.

Schools are not required to find that a child has a severe discrepancy between achievement and intellectual ability before determining that the child has a specific learning disability and needs special education and related services. Schools are allowed to use a process to determine if the child responds to scientific, research-based intervention as a part of the evaluation process.[13]

---

provide them with appropriate research-based instruction. Schools are to provide research-based interventions (tiers) designed to meet each child's needs. The child's progress is monitored often. Educational decisions about intensity and duration of interventions are based on data from progress monitoring.

If struggling learners receive appropriate research-based instruction early, many will not need special education services. Decisions about whether to move a child to a more intensive level or tier are based on data from testing and progress monitoring.[14]

With Response to Intervention, the devil is in the details. Many RTI models are available.

All About Tests and Assessments

Research on the effectiveness of RTI models is limited. States use different guidelines to implement RTI. School districts within states use different frameworks. Some districts refuse to follow their state guidelines on RTI.

RTI requires teachers who are trained to provide scientific, research-based interventions. Many districts are likely to have difficulty locating or training these teachers.

After the law was changed to include RTI, schools began using RTI to deny or delay evaluating children who may have disabilities and need special education.[15]

My child is in RTI. He is not making progress. The school will not refer him for a special education evaluation until he stays in RTI for several months. Is this legal?

No. If you request a comprehensive evaluation to determine if your child is eligible for special education services, the school is required to evaluate and determine eligibility. The fact that your child is in RTI does not change this legal requirement.[16]

In 2011, the U.S. Department of Education published a Memorandum clarifying that schools may not use RTI to delay or deny providing a comprehensive evaluation for special education.[17]

The school may use information about your child's progress or lack of progress in RTI as part of the evaluation process. The school may *not* use RTI to delay or deny a comprehensive evaluation. [18]

One of my students was diagnosed with dyslexia in first grade. He has been receiving RTI for over a year with no evidence of progress. The team refuses to evaluate him. What can I do?

As a teacher, you can refer a student for a comprehensive evaluation at any time. You should also share your concerns with the child's parents. The parents need to know they can refer their child for an evaluation too.

Resources

National Research Center on Learning Disabilities. (2005, July). *Responsiveness to intervention in the SLD determination process.* Washington, D.C.: U.S. Department of Education. Retrieved from www.osepideasthatwork.org/toolkit/pdf/RTI_SLD.pdf

Klotz, M, & Canter, A. (n.d.). *Response to Intervention (RTI): A primer for parents.* Bethesda, MD: National Association of School Psychologists. Retrieved from www.nasponline.org/resources/factsheets/rtiprimer.aspx

Hale, J. (2008). *Response to Intervention: Guidelines for parents and practitioners.* Retrieved from www.wrightslaw.com/idea/art/rti.hale.pdf

U.S. Office of Special Education Programs. (2003). *Identifying and treating attention deficit hyperactivity disorder: A resource for school and home.* Washington, D.C.: U.S. Department of Education. Retrieved from www2.ed.gov/teachers/needs/speced/adhd/adhd-resource-pt1.doc

In Summation

In this chapter, you learned about evaluating children with specific learning disabilities and Attention-Deficit/Hyperactivity Disorder (ADHD). You learned about executive functioning skills and how they are assessed. You learned the legal requirements for specific learning disabilities and the role of Response to Intervention in the evaluation process.

Let's move on to Chapter 11 where you will learn about assessments of hearing, vision, and motor skills.

Endnotes

1. Sattler, J. M. and R. D. Hoge. (2005). *Assessment of children: cognitive foundations* (5th ed.). San Diego, CA: author

2. 20 U.S.C. §1414(c)(1)(A), 34 C.F.R. §300.310

3. 20 U.S.C. §1221e-3; 1401(30); 1414(b)(6), 34 C.F.R. §300.310(c)

4. American Psychiatric Association. (2013). *Diagnostic and statistical manual of mental disorders (5th ed.)*. Arlington, VA: American Psychiatric Publishing

5. 20 U.S.C. §1401(30), 34 C.F.R. §300.8(c)(10)

6. 20 U.S.C. §1414(c)

7. 34 C.F.R. §300.8(c)

8. 34 C.F.R. §300.101(c)

9. U.S. Office of Special Education Programs. (2003). *Identifying and treating attention deficit hyperactivity disorder: A resource for school and home*. Washington, D.C.: U.S. Department of Education. Retrieved from www2.ed.gov/teachers/needs/speced/adhd/adhd-resource-pt1.doc

10. The *DSM-V* specifies age 12. The American Academy of Pediatrics specifies age 4 in the article, *ADHD: Clinical Practice Guideline for the Diagnosis, Evaluation, and Treatment of Attention-Deficit Hyperactivity Disorder in Children and Adolescents* retrieved from www.pediatrics.aapublications.org/content/early/2011/10/14/peds.2011-2654.full.pdf + html

11. G.A. Gioia, P.K. Isquith, L. Kenworthy, & R.M. Barton (2000). *Behavior Rating Inventory of Executive Functioning (BRIEF) Manual*. Odessa, FL: Psychological Assessment Resources

12. www.ncld.org/types-learning-disabilities/executive-function-disorders/what-is-executive-function

13. 20 U.S.C. §1414(b)(6)

14. National Center on Learning Disabilities. *What is RTI?* Retrieved from www.rtinetwork.org/learn/what/whatisrti

15. U.S. Department of Education. (2011). *A Response to Intervention process cannot be used to delay-deny an evaluation for eligibility under the IDEA* (OSEP 11-07). Retrieved from: www.wrightslaw.com/info/rti.osep.memo.0111.pdf

16. 20 U.S.C. §1414(a)(1)

17. U.S. Department of Education. (2011). *A Response to Intervention process cannot be used to delay-deny an evaluation for eligibility under the IDEA* (OSEP 11-07). Retrieved from: www.wrightslaw.com/info/rti.osep.memo.0111.pdf

18. 34 C.F.R. §300.307(a)(2) and *Responsiveness to Intervention in the SLD Process* published by the U.S. Department of Education. Retrieved from www.osepideasthatwork.org/toolkit/pdf/RTI_SLD.pdf

Assessments of Hearing, Vision, and Motor Skills

- Assessing Hearing Impairments

- Assessing Vision Impairments

- Assessing Motor Skills

- Assistive Technology Assessments

If your child has impaired sensory or motor skills, you can expect him to have difficulty learning. Some children have sensory impairments that affect both vision and hearing.

Assessing the hearing and vision of a child with sensory impairments brings special challenges. The child may not understand what the examiner asks him, or he may not be able to answer questions in the usual way. The evaluator should have expertise in communication and mobility, and experience in assessing children with sensory impairments.

All About Tests and Assessments

In this chapter, you will learn about assessing sensory impairments—hearing, vision, and motor skills. You will also learn about assistive technology (AT) —the devices and services that use technology to improve your child's ability to learn and function.

Assessing Hearing Impairments

Hearing impairment is a term that describes hearing losses that affect your child's educational performance.[1] A hearing loss ranges from mild to profound.

The descriptors *mild, moderate, severe,* or *profound* may not accurately describe the impact that the hearing loss has on your child in the classroom. Even a mild hearing loss can have a profound impact on your child's ability to learn, especially if the loss is undetected.

When should I have my child screened for hearing problems?

It is never too early to have your child's hearing screened. Ask your child's doctor or the school to perform the screening.

A hearing screening is a thumbs-up or a thumbs-down test. If your child passes the screening, he is presumed to have normal hearing. If he does not pass the screening, he needs to be referred to a pediatric audiologist for a comprehensive hearing evaluation. Since hearing loss can be progressive, it is a good idea to have your child's hearing screened annually.

If your child has a history of ear infections, speech delays, or trouble learning, he should have a hearing evaluation. An unidentified, untreated hearing loss causes language delays and behavioral problems.

The audiologist can show you how to improve your child's hearing in school and at home.

My child is scheduled for a hearing assessment. What should we expect?

The hearing assessment will be conducted by an audiologist. The audiologist will ask questions about your child's medical history and hearing. A hearing assessment seeks to answer these questions:

- What is the degree of the hearing loss?

- What is the type of hearing loss?

- What are the characteristics of the hearing loss?

The assessment is in a soundproofed room. Your child will wear earphones and will signal what he hears by pressing a button or by raising a finger to signal "yes." The audiologist will use several tests and will plot your child's responses on a graph called an audiogram.

An audiologist advised us that our daughter has a mild-to-moderate hearing loss. Should we be concerned?

Yes, you should be concerned. There are four levels of hearing loss:

- Mild (26 to 40 dB)

- Moderate (41 to 70 dB)

- Severe (71 to 90 dB)

- Profound (91+ dB)

Language delay, speech impairment, and gaps in communication and understanding occur at all levels of hearing loss. The greater the hearing loss, the more risk in all areas.

A child with a mild hearing loss will have difficulty listening to teachers, participating in discussions, and following directions. A mild loss makes it hard to discern speech sounds in words.

Your daughter's mild-to-moderate hearing loss means she does not hear the "s" sound in speech—and "s" is a very important sound to miss! The "s" sound tells us whether we have one thing or many things. Imagine not knowing if you had more than one assignment due!

The audiogram in Figure 11-1 gives you an idea of the frequency (pitch) and volume of common sounds. A jackhammer is a loud,

Figure 11-1. Audiogram of Familiar Sounds [1]

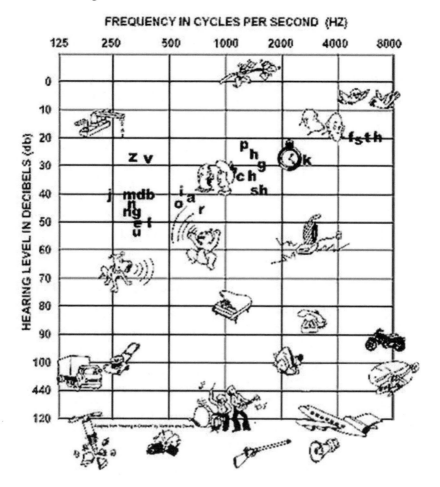

low sound. A bird's tweet is a soft, high sound. The sounds of speech range between 250 to 5000 Hz. A typical conversation occurs around 40 dB. The greater the hearing loss, the more difficult it is to understand what people are saying.

My child has a severe hearing loss. He is having a comprehensive special education evaluation. How should we prepare for this evaluation?

Children who are deaf and hard of hearing are a diverse group. As a parent, you are an invaluable source of information for the evaluator.

The evaluator needs to know the type of hearing loss, degree of loss, and age of onset. She needs to know about your child's language skills, how he receives information, and how he communicates. You are the best source of information about your child's communication skills.[2]

If your child wears a hearing aid, the evaluator may ask when it was last checked, whether your child uses it consistently, and if it is turned on. She may inquire about your child's good ear and where she should sit. She needs to know about your child's FM amplification system and how to use it during testing. Some children enjoy teaching their evaluator about their FM systems.

Standardized tests designed for children with normal hearing are likely to present problems for your child with a hearing impairment. Many intelligence tests include measures of vocabulary and verbal reasoning. It is not appropriate to use tests that presume hearing with a child who has a hearing impairment.

My child has a hearing impairment and communication problems. Will the evaluator understand him?

Many children with hearing impairments also have communication problems. Your child may have difficulty when the examiner describes test directions. Tests with oral instructions may not be appropriate, even if the tasks are visual.

In these cases, the examiner should use nonverbal tests that do not assume hearing ability. If your child uses a technology like a high-powered hearing aid or a cochlear implant to listen and speak, he may still need to be evaluated with nonverbal tests. See Chapter 4 to learn about nonverbal intelligence tests.

If your child communicates with sign language, the evaluator should use an interpreter who uses the same form of sign language as the child, speaks English, and is trained in assessment.

Assessing Vision Impairments

Your child needs good near vision (10 to 13 inches) and good distance vision to learn in the classroom. She must be able to adjust her focus to accommodate changes in distance and to use both eyes together.

She needs to see objects in her peripheral vision (on the side) while looking ahead. She needs to coordinate her hands with what her eyes see (visual-motor skill).

Children with vision impairments are classified into three groups.

- The child's vision is not useful in the test situation.

- The child can use vision to manage large objects but cannot use vision to read, even with large print.

- The child can use vision to read only if print is large, or with a magnifier or other aid.

After the school screened my child's vision, they recommended that she have a comprehensive vision examination. What should I know about vision examinations?

Since your child did not pass the vision screening, she needs a thorough examination by an optometrist or ophthalmologist. The doctor will ask you about your child's health history, family history, and vision issues. He will perform tests to measure your child's visual acuity and how her eyes function.

My child has pediatric glaucoma with severe vision loss. The school wants to evaluate her for special education services. What should we know about this evaluation?

The assessment should be comprehensive and assess your child's intellectual, academic, social/emotional, and physical skills.

Schedule a meeting with the examiner to discuss your child and the evaluation ahead of time. The examiner needs to know about your child's visual impairment to design the evaluation and select appropriate tests. Describe your child's useable vision and her field of vision.

Ask the examiner to assess your child in at least one familiar setting. The examiner should provide your child with time to acclimate to an unfamiliar environment. The evaluation may be spaced over several shorter sessions to reduce the impact of fatigue.

My daughter is blind. The school wants to administer a standardized IQ test that is not designed for blind children. Can I ask the school not to use this IQ test?

Although the test was not designed for blind children, it may be permissible to use the test with blind children. Test publishers provide instructions about how to administer their tests. You may be able to find information online about who may be tested with this test.

Discuss your concerns and questions with the examiner. The examiner needs to select tests that allow your child to show what she knows —tests that measure your child's abilities, not her impaired skills.

If your child has a visual impairment, it is not appropriate to use tests that presume good vision. Information from you will help the examiner decide what tests to administer.

I teach children who are visually impaired. What should I know about assessing a child who has a visual impairment?

If a child has visual impairments, he may have difficulty on classroom tasks that involve pictures. He may not be able to interpret graphs, charts, and other information presented visually.

If the child's visual impairment is significant, the tests given in class should not rely on vision. A specialist or consultant for the blind and visually impaired can suggest appropriate tests and classroom strategies.

Factors to Consider When Assessing a Child with Sensory Impairments

A child with a sensory impairment may:

- Fatigue easily

- Require frequent breaks

- Have difficulty sustaining attention

- Not be able to finish timed tests

- Not be able to sit for long periods of time

- Have difficulty with sitting-balance, maintaining posture, arm-hand use

- Have trouble answering questions; indicating "yes" or "no"

- Be able to point or use eye gaze

- Have an effective mode of communication

Before evaluating your child with sensory or motor impairments, the examiner should observe your child's vision, hearing, and speech, and become familiar with your child's ability to respond. The examiner will be able to select appropriate tests based on your child's strengths and limitations.[3]

Assessing Motor Skills

A child may have motor skill deficits from a birth defect, developmental disability, illness, or injury.

Evaluating a child with impaired motor skills requires a high degree of expertise. The evaluator's ability to do the assessment may be limited by the child's impaired motor skills. You should view test results with caution.

My child has cerebral palsy. He is being evaluated for special education. What do I need to know about the evaluation?

The evaluation must assess all areas related to your child's suspected disability. See Chapter 2, Evaluations by the School.

Since your child has cerebral palsy, his motor, speech, visual, and auditory difficulties are likely to limit the use of standardized tests. It is not appropriate to use tests with time limits for children with weak motor skills unless the goal is to measure speed of performance.

If your child has good hand use and poor speech, the examiner may use tests that do not require expressive language. If he has poor hand use and good speech, the examiner may use verbal tests.

My child has spina bifida and needs physical therapy (PT). When I asked the team to add physical therapy to her IEP, they scheduled a physical therapy evaluation. What should I know about PT evaluations?

A physical therapy evaluation should include background history, information from interviews of parents and teachers, standardized tests, and observations. The evaluation may assess:

- Motor skills including reflexes, coordination, balance

- Gait (how she walks)

- Need for specialized equipment (e.g., wheelchair or walker, assistive devices)

In the Individuals with Disabilities Education Act (IDEA), physical therapy is a related service that should be included in your child's IEP.[4]

If the school is evaluating your child for physical therapy services, the evaluation will focus on her performance in the school environment. For example, the physical therapist may evaluate your child's ability to move around the school and participate in classroom activities. School physical therapists can ensure that your child has access to educational activities, school play, and recreation.

Physical therapists also screen, evaluate, and assess toddlers to identify problems with movement. They gather information to prevent or compensate for movement

dysfunction and other functional problems in older children.

Commonly used tests include the *Peabody Developmental Motor Scales, Second Edition* and the *Bruininks-Oseretsky Test of Motor Proficiency, Second Edition.*

Who does physical therapy evaluations?

Physical therapists conduct physical therapy evaluations. Because physical therapists have expertise in assistive technology, transition, and vocational training, a physical therapist can be an invaluable member of your child's team.

How can an occupational therapist help?

An occupational therapist can assess your child's:

- Handwriting and keyboarding skills

- Fine motor skills

- Eye-hand coordination

- Visual perceptual skills

- Organizational skills

- Sensory Processing

An occupational therapist (OT) wears many hats. She may help with proper seating for a child who has difficulty maintaining good posture in a chair. She may develop programs to help a child improve motor planning skills so he can carry out multistep tasks.

An OT can help the school team design accommodations so a child can use information presented on a blackboard or copy that information onto a sheet of paper. Occupational therapists may also assess handwriting. See Chapter 7, Writing and Spelling Assessments.

Occupational therapists (OT) administer tests including the *Peabody Developmental Motor Scales* and the *Bruininks Oseretsky Developmental Test of Motor Proficiency* to learn about the child's gross and fine motor functioning.

Occupational therapists also administer tests of visual perceptual and visual-motor skills like the *Beery Buktenica Developmental Test of Visual-Motor Integration, Sixth Edition.*

My child has learning disabilities and an IEP. He has fine motor deficits. His handwriting is illegible. He has difficulty getting organized and completing homework assignments. Can I ask the school to provide help with handwriting and organizational skills?

Yes. Be sure to put your request for an evaluation in writing!

Your child may also benefit from an assistive technology assessment. A keyboarding assessment by an assistive technology specialist will provide information about devices that will limit or eliminate the fine-motor skills required in typing.

After an evaluation, the OT will consult with you and school staff to develop a plan that may include modifications to the environment at home and/or school. The OT may select assistive and orthotic devices (e.g., braces, splints) to help your child with handwriting.

Occupational therapy is a related service. Related services are developmental, corrective, and other supportive services to help a child with a disability benefit from special education.[5]

Assistive Technology Assessments

Assistive technology (AT) includes devices and services to improve your child's ability to function and learn. AT allows the child to use his strengths to compensate or work around the weaknesses caused by his disability.

The Individuals with Disabilities Education Act (IDEA) requires IEP teams to consider the assistive technology needs of **all** children with disabilities.[6]

Assistive technology assessments focus on three areas:

- Computer access and/or written expression

- Environmental control

- Augmentative communication

In an assistive technology assessment, an AT specialist interviews parents and teachers. The specialist observes the child at home and in other settings.

Some AT specialists use questionnaires like the *Functional Evaluation for Assistive*

Technology (FEAT). The *FEAT* has five scales for members of the child's AT team to complete. The *FEAT* helps AT specialists make recommendations that meet the unique needs of a particular child.

My child has autism and does not speak. He needs a communication system.

Children and adults who have severe speech or language problems use augmentative and alternative communication (AAC) systems to supplement or replace speech. These systems can help your child communicate, interact socially, and learn. AAC includes:

- Picture and symbol boards
- Voice recognition
- Speech synthesis devices

Information from an assistive technology evaluation will help you and the AT select an augmentative and alternative communication (AAC) system.

You may also want to consult with a speech language pathologist (SLP) about augmentative and alternative communication systems.

In Summation

In this chapter, you learned about tests used to assess the hearing, vision, and motor disorders that can affect your child's ability to learn. You also learned about physical therapy, occupational therapy, and assistive technology evaluations.

Let's move on to Chapter 12 to explore processing disorders.

Resources

Differences Between Hearing Screening and Hearing Evaluation. Retrieved from www.asha.org/public/hearing/Hearing-Testing/

Types of Tests Used to Evaluate Hearing in Children and Adults. Retrieved from www. asha.org/public/hearing/Types-of-Tests-Used-to-Evaluate-Hearing/

Occupational Therapy Assessment Strategies. Retrieved from http://depts.washington.edu/lend/seminars/modules/ot/otpractice_strategies.htm

C.S. Kranowitz. (2005). *Sensory Processing Disorder.* Retrieved from www.smartkidswithld.org/ld-basics/evaluation-diagnosis/sensory-processing-disorder

Endnotes

1. Courtesy of Leeanne Seaver, Hands and Voices. www.handsandvoices.org

34 C.F.R. §300.8(c)(5)

2. Ibid.

3. Sattler, J.M. (2008). *Assessment of Children: Cognitive foundations (5th ed.).* San Diego CA: Author

4. 20 U.S.C. §1401(26), 34 C.F.R. §300.34(c)

5. 20 U.S.C. §1401(26), 34 C.F.R. §300.34(c)(6)

6. 20 U.S.C. §1414(d)(3)(B)(v)

Auditory, Visual, Visual-Motor, and Sensory Processing Assessments

- Assessing Auditory Processing Disorders

- Assessing Visual Processing Disorders

- Assessing Visual-Motor Skills and Dyspraxia

- Assessing Sensory Processing Disorders

Your brain uses sight, hearing, smell, taste, and touch to gather information. A **processing disorder** refers to a problem in the way your brain interprets information from your senses. A processing disorder is not related to intelligence. The most common conditions are auditory, visual, visual-motor, and sensory processing disorders.

If your child has an auditory processing disorder, he is likely to have trouble distinguishing sounds and understanding language, even though he has normal hearing. If your child has a visual processing disorder, he may struggle to see the difference between similar letters, shapes, or objects.

If your child has a sensory processing disorder, she may be easily overloaded by what she sees, hears, feels, tastes, and smells.

Assessing Auditory Processing Disorders

Auditory processing is how your child's brain makes sense of what he hears. An auditory processing disorder is a weakness in how the brain interprets or processes auditory information.

A child with an auditory processing disorder will have weaknesses in some or all of the following areas:

- **Auditory Figure-Ground Problems** make it difficult for your child to focus on what he needs to hear when there is background noise. Although we think of classrooms as a quiet places, they are filled with the sounds of heating systems, chairs shuffling, children talking, and noise from the street. These sounds compete with the teacher's voice.

- **Auditory Memory Problems** make it hard for your child to follow directions and learn during lectures and discussions.

- **Auditory Discrimination Problems** affect your child's ability to perceive sounds in words. Poor sound discrimination will affect his ability to learn to read and spell, and make it difficult to understand spoken language.

- **Auditory Attention Problems** can compromise your child's ability to focus

during long tasks that require him to listen. He may perceive a teacher's lecture as an endless stream of "blah, blah, blah."

- **Auditory Cohesion Problems** involve tasks that require verbal reasoning.

My daughter has difficulty remembering and following directions. Her hearing is fine. Her doctor says she needs to be tested for an auditory processing disorder. What do we need to know about this assessment?

If your child has an auditory processing disorder (APD), she will have difficulty listening, following directions, and hearing speech in noisy environments.[1] She may also have trouble learning to spell, read, and understanding information presented verbally. Even though a child with an auditory processing disorder tries to pay attention, she will miss much of what her teachers and friends say.

Auditory processing skills are assessed with intellectual assessments and language tests. The *Test of Auditory Processing Skills, Third Edition (TAPS-3)* is designed to assess how well your child understands what she hears.

If you suspect that your child has a hearing loss or an auditory processing deficit, she needs to have auditory testing before she is assessed with the *TAPS-3*[2]. Attention problems should also be ruled out before she is tested.

Although a symptom checklist may be helpful, an auditory processing disorder cannot be diagnosed with a checklist alone.

Who evaluates auditory processing disorders in children?

Pediatric audiologists evaluate auditory processing and other hearing disorders. The audiologist will assess your child's hearing in a soundproofed room. The audiologist will ask your child to listen and respond to sounds. He will test sounds in quiet and in noise, and will assess your child's ability to discriminate sound sequences and patterns.

After the evaluation, the audiologist may discuss treatments and interventions. Interventions include modifying the environment, teaching compensatory strategies, and auditory training.

My child has frequent ear infections. Can ear infections cause an auditory processing disorder?

Yes, auditory processing disorders may result from ear infections, a head injury, or neuro-developmental delays.

A child who has chronic ear infections can have listening difficulties for weeks or months after the infection passes.[3] If your child has frequent ear infections, he needs an evaluation by an audiologist. See Chapter 11 for Assessments of Hearing and Vision.

Assessing Visual Processing Disorders

Visual processing refers to how your child's brain makes sense of what his eyes see. Visual processing is not the same as sight. Visual processing disorders are also called visual perceptual disorders.

My child has 20/20 vision but the teacher says she struggles with visual processing.

If your child has visual processing weaknesses, this will affect her ability to perform in school. She may have difficulties with:

- Copying from books or the board

- Working with graphs and charts

- Writing on a line or within margins

- Following directions and schedules

- Writing coherent, well-organized essays

- Understanding place value and fractions

- Telling time and reading maps

- Organizing thoughts, materials, and possessions

How is visual processing assessed?

A visual processing assessment includes tests of your child's skills in several areas.

- **Visual discrimination tests** require him to distinguish between symbols and to identify symbols that are alike or different.

- **Visual short-term memory tests** measure his ability to recall geometric shapes or pictures after a short delay.

- **Visual sequential tests** assess whether he can remember shapes and/or pictures in the order presented.

- **Visual figure-ground tests** require him to find /identify important details within a complex visual or busy background.

- **Visual-spatial relations tasks** require him to picture how the parts of a puzzle form a whole, or analyze and reproduce a complex design.

- **Visual-motor tests** require him to coordinate his hands with what he sees. On visual-motor tests, the examiner may ask him to copy geometric designs and draw designs from memory. He may have to arrange items or blocks in a particular orientation, or follow a path with a pencil while staying within the lines.

Commonly used tests of visual perception and visual-motor ability include:

- The *Beery Buktenica Developmental Test of Visual-Motor Integration, Sixth Edition*

- The *Motor Free Visual Perception Test, Third Edition*

- The *Developmental Test of Visual Perception, Third Edition*

These tests may be administered by occupational therapists, neuropsychologists, and psychologists, and by school psychologists and learning disabilities specialists.

Assessing Visual-Motor Skills and Dyspraxia

My child was diagnosed with dyspraxia. What is dyspraxia?

Dyspraxia is a neurological condition that affects fine motor skills. Dyspraxia is also called Developmental Coordination Disorder (DCD). Dyspraxia is not a specific learning disability, but often exists with learning disabilities and other conditions that affect your child's ability to learn.

How does dyspraxia affect my child's ability to learn?

When your child has dyspraxia, he will have difficulty planning and completing motor tasks. He may be clumsy and accident-prone and his speech may be affected. Writing will be difficult.

Who can evaluate a child for dyspraxia?

Medical professionals, psychologists, and occupational therapists evaluate and diagnose dyspraxia, often with help from speech and language therapists and physical therapists.

What should I know about my child's evaluation for dyspraxia?

The evaluator will obtain your child's developmental history, including delays in motor skills and language.

The evaluation should include a neurological evaluation to rule out other conditions, including cerebral palsy. The evaluator should investigate other conditions that often occur with dyspraxia, including ADHD, speech and language impairments, and specific learning disabilities.

Dyspraxia or Developmental Coordination Disorder cannot be diagnosed with a single test. The examiner may use the *Bruininks-Oseretsky Test of Motor Proficiency, Second Edition* and a checklist like the *Developmental*

Coordination Disorder Questionnaire, Revised as part of the evaluation.

My son was evaluated with the *Rey-Osterrieth Complex Figure Test* that required him to copy a design. The evaluator said he is "disorganized." What does this mean?

The *Rey-Osterrieth Complex Figure Test (ROCF)* is a neuropsychological-type test that assesses spatial skills, organization, and planning. Evaluators who are trained to do cognitive assessments administer the *ROCF*.

When your child is tested with the *ROCF*, the examiner will ask your child to copy a design with pencil and paper. The examiner scores the design for accuracy and observes how your child works.

The key to understanding this test is **structure**. The design is highly structured. Your child has to make decisions about important parts of the design and less important details.

An "organized" child begins with the important parts. He makes decisions in the same way that a builder constructs a building. The frame goes up before doors and windows. An organized child knows how the shapes of the design fit together so his copied design is accurate.

A "disorganized" child may not see how shapes fit together and what is important. He may not know how to plan and complete a complicated task. He may also have difficulty

grouping ideas and facts into logical units—like paragraphs. His writing may be cluttered with details.

Assessing Sensory Processing Disorders

Is your child clumsy, fidgety, and overly sensitive? Does he have difficulties with speech, fine-motor skills, and coordination?

If the answer to these questions is "yes," your child may have a sensory processing disorder.

Sensory processing disorder is a general term for many neurological or brain-based conditions. Sensory processing disorders exist when sensory signals do not get organized into appropriate responses.

Sensory processing disorders (SPD) are often described as "neurological traffic jams." The brain does not receive the information needed to interpret sensory information correctly.

A child with SPD has difficulty processing and acting on information received through the senses. This creates difficulty performing countless everyday tasks. The child is likely to have motor clumsiness, anxiety, depression, low self-esteem, and social isolation. He is at risk for emotional, social, and educational problems if he does not receive effective treatment.[4]

If your child is like many children with sensory processing problems, he may also have behavioral problems.[5]

All About Tests and Assessments

My child is scheduled for a sensory processing evaluation. What should I know about this evaluation?

A sensory processing evaluation will assess your child's ability to take in, process, and respond to stimuli from the environment. If your child cannot efficiently process information through his senses (vision, hearing, taste, smell, touch, or movement), he is likely to have problems at school.

The evaluation should include standardized and informal testing, observations, and interviews with the child's parents and teachers. The examiner may use questionnaires to determine how your child handles the sensory demands of different settings.

Symptoms of sensory processing disorder can be mistaken for other conditions, including ADHD, learning disabilities, auditory or visual processing difficulties, and emotional problems.

A comprehensive evaluation should include vision and hearing tests. Based on information from the evaluation, the evaluator may recommend strategies to increase your child's tolerance of different sensations.

Who conducts sensory processing evaluations?

Occupational and physical therapists who are specially trained in sensory integrative disorders conduct sensory processing evaluations.

Diagnoses of sensory processing disorders or sensory integration dysfunctions are controversial. Sensory processing disorders are not included in the *Diagnostic and Statistical Manual of Mental Disorders, Fifth Edition (DSM-V)*, or the diagnostic system used by the World Health Organization.

Resources

Sensory Processing Disorder Checklist: Signs and Symptoms
www.sensory-processing-disorder.com/sensory-processing-disorder-checklist.html

Symptoms of Sensory Integration Dysfunction
www.sensory-processing-disorder.com/sensory-integration-dysfunction-symptoms.html

---

In Summation

In this chapter, you learned about auditory, visual, visual motor, and sensory processing disorders and how these conditions are assessed.

It's time to move on to Chapter 13 where you'll learn about behavior assessments.

Endnotes

1. Bellis, T.J. *Understanding Auditory Processing Disorders in Children.* Retrieved from www.asha.org/public/hearing/Understanding-Auditory-Processing-Disorders-in-Children/

2. Martin, N., & Brownell, R. (2005). *Test of Auditory Processing Skills, Third Edition Manual.* Novato, CA: Academic Therapy Publications

3. Willis, J. (1998). Post-otitis auditory dysfunction. *NHASP Protocol. Newsletter of the NH assoc. of School Psychologists,* 17(1), 6-7, 9

4. Sensory Processing Disorder Foundation. *About Sensory Processing Disorders.* www. spdfoundation.net/about-sensory-processing-disorder.html

5. Kranowitz, C.S. *Sensory Processing Disorder.* Retrieved from www.smartkidswithld.org/ld-basics/evaluation-diagnosis/sensory-processing-disorder

Adaptive Behavior and Functional Behavior Assessments

- Adaptive Behavior Assessments
- Functional Behavior Assessments (FBAs)

If your child has a disability, he may have behaviors that make it difficult for him to learn. These behaviors may be harmful to him and others and may cause other children to avoid him.

A functional behavioral assessment (FBA) is designed to help your child's team and his teachers understand his behaviors and the purpose they serve. His team can use this information to develop a plan to teach him replacement behaviors that will meet his needs.

Adaptive behavior is a term for the skills your child needs to live safely and independently in the community. In this chapter, you will learn

about adaptive behavior, functional behavior, and the behavior scales and behavioral checklists that are used to identify strengths and weaknesses.

Adaptive Behavior Assessments

Adaptive behavior includes:

- Communication skills

- Academic skills

- Daily living or independent functioning skills

- Social skills

What is an adaptive behavior assessment?

An adaptive behavior assessment is used to determine if your child has the age-appropriate skills he needs to live safely and independently and participate in the community.

Typically, an adaptive behavior assessment includes questionnaires and interviews with parents, teachers, and social workers. The evaluator may also interview your child. The evaluation often includes observations of your child at home, in school, and in the community or workplace.

Who can do adaptive behavior assessments?

Evaluators and teachers conduct adaptive behavior assessments. Your child may display different behaviors and skills in different settings. An adaptive behavior assessment should include information from parents,

teachers, and others who know your child. The examiner will use behavior scales and checklists to obtain information from these responders.

Typically, parents rate the child's behavior at home (e.g., eating, sleeping, recreation, self-help, relations with siblings and other family members). Teachers rate behaviors that occur at school (e.g., attention, academic performance, peer relations). A vocational counselor may rate behaviors that occur in the workplace. All perspectives are helpful in obtaining an accurate picture of your child.

Part of the evaluator's job is to assess each respondent's credibility. All respondents will not agree on how a child presents, what he does, or how often he displays a particular behavior. Some respondents may minimize or exaggerate the child's behaviors. The child may behave differently in different environments.

Is there one good test that measures adaptive behavior?

No test measures all areas of adaptive behavior. The examiner should select appropriate adaptive behavior scales and/or behavioral checklists for your child.

Dozens of adaptive behavior scales and behavioral checklists are available. Some measure a few broad factors (e.g., conduct problem, personality problem, immaturity). Others measure many factors (for example, hyperactivity, withdrawal, aggression).

Adaptive behavior scales and checklists differ in the responses they require. Some have two responses ("yes" or "no," "true" or "false"). Others require informants to rank responses (for example, on a scale of 1-5). Ratings may be based on a specified time period ("How often was the child aggressive within the last week?") or no time period ("How aggressive is the child?").

The *Assessment of Basic Language and Learning Skills, Revised (ABLLS-R)* is designed to measure language, self-help, social interaction, academic, and motor skills in children who are on the autism spectrum. It can be used to measure progress and as a guide for instruction.

The *Adaptive Behavior Assessment System-Second Edition (ABAS-II)* uses a rating format to document skills in the home, school, workplace, and community. The *ABAS-II* rates health, self-care, safety, academics, communication, social interaction, and self-direction skills.

The school used the *Vineland Adaptive Behavior Scales, Second Edition*, as part of my daughter's assessment. I asked for the parent/caregiver form. The team said only the teacher fills out a form. Is this correct?

No. The purpose of an adaptive behavior assessment is learn if your child has the skills she needs to live independently, participate in school and the community, and function in the workplace. To answer these questions, the assessment must document her behaviors and skills in different settings. If the examiner only assesses your child's adaptive behavior skills at school, the assessment will not accomplish its purpose.

The *Vineland Adaptive Behavior Scales, Second Edition* provides different ways to learn about your child's abilities. The "Survey Interview Form" can be completed by anyone who is familiar with your child and her behavior. If the child lives at home, her parents are usually the most appropriate respondents.[1]

If it is difficult to schedule a face-to-face interview with the child's parents, the examiner can use the "Parent/Caregiver Form." The parents complete a checklist and rate the skills and behaviors they observe.

The *Vineland* also includes a "Teacher Rating Form" of behaviors in the classroom that does not request information about the child's self-care and daily living skills.

How can I prepare for my child's adaptive behavior assessment?

The scope of the adaptive behavior assessment depends on your child. The interviewer may use rating scales and checklists that are objective and easy to score. These tests ask parents, teachers, and sometimes the child, to indicate the presence and degree of different behaviors.

Answer the questions openly and honestly. Describe what your child **does**, not what he "can do." It is helpful if you provide the interviewer with examples of your child's skills and behaviors, and examples of your concerns about your child's limitations.

If you do not understand a question, ask the interviewer to clarify what the question means.

Functional Behavior Assessments (FBAs)

Your child may have behaviors that are difficult for him to control. A child with autism or a developmental disability, for example, may have self-injurious behaviors. Your child may not know how to ask for help. A child with a communication disorder may use behavior to communicate his wants, needs, and fears.

What is a functional behavior assessment (FBA)?

A functional behavior assessment (FBA) is based on the assumption that problem behaviors serve a purpose for your child. An FBA is the process of collecting information about these behaviors. The information collected is used to determine why a behavior happens, the purpose it serves, and to develop a plan to change it.

In an FBA, a behaviorist or behavior specialist will observe your child in different settings, depending on where the behavior occurs or does **not** occur—in the classroom, the cafeteria, the playground, and at home. She will observe the frequency, duration, intensity, rate, and location of the behavior.

The behavior specialist should interview you, your child, and your child's teachers. She should review your child's records and assessments, and may use tests or checklists to gather information.

This process will lead the behavior specialist to a hypothesis or educated guess about what triggers the behavior and what purpose it serves. Your child's team will use this information to develop a positive behavior intervention plan.

Positive behavioral interventions should be used *before* problem behaviors occur.

Who can do functional behavior assessments?

Behavior specialists and behaviorists are trained to record and analyze data and make recommendations based on their findings. These specialists use knowledge of psychology, learning disorders and disabilities, communication, and special education to design plans to teach and reinforce positive behaviors.

Behavior specialists are trained to work with special populations, including children with autism or intellectual disabilities.

In some states, behavior specialists are licensed mental health professionals. Other states do not have licensure requirements for behavior specialists.

Shouldn't bad behaviors be punished?

The way most people deal with problem behaviors is based on their personal beliefs.

Some people believe that the *child is a problem*. Others believe that the *child has a problem*.

Many of your child's behaviors are not bad or good. Behavior is often an attempt to reduce anxiety. Problem behaviors occur when your child is feeling stressed and cannot effectively communicate his needs to others.

Your child does not always know why she is upset or that she is not paying attention.

A behavior problem in the classroom may be triggered by noise and activities within the classroom. Think about it. When your child is trying to pay attention to the teacher, she must filter out the noise and activity of 20 or more students, visual and outside distractions, and background noises. This can lead to sensory overload.

Your child may be confused or anxious if the classroom lacks structure. She may get upset when events or plans change unexpectedly (e.g., a substitute teacher, class party).

Sometimes, school is just too hard. Your child may not have the skills needed to do the work she is required to do. She may use off task or inappropriate behaviors to escape from a setting or an assignment that is unpleasant or impossible.

What do behavior specialists look for when conducting an FBA?

The behavior specialist will look for positive and negative behaviors. She will observe how the child responds to academic or other difficulties or successes. She will look for information about:

- When, where, and with whom does this behavior most commonly occur?
- How often, how long, how intense is the behavior?
- What is typically happening before the behavior occurs?
- What typically happens after the behavior?
- Does the child have the academic skills needed to do the assigned work?
- What are other children doing?
- What does the teacher do after the behavior occurs?
- What do the other children do after the behavior occurs?
- What interventions are in place now?
- What interventions have been tried in the past?
- What has or has not worked to modify the target behaviors?

The behavior specialist will observe the classroom environment.

- Is the classroom arranged to limit distractions, background noise, and interruptions?
- Are traffic patterns clearly defined?
- Is the child's seating in the classroom conducive to prompt attention from the teacher?

- How many students, teachers, and aides are in the classroom?

- Are class rules and consequences, and the daily schedule of activities posted?

After the specialist collects information and defines the behavior that needs to be addressed, the child's team will design a positive Behavior Intervention Plan to decrease stressful events or situations.

The child's behavior will not change until the environment changes. Typically, a behavior intervention plan calls for changes in the behavior of adults.

A behavior plan is not about punishment. A behavior plan should provide alternative behaviors and teach new skills so the child can respond to stressful events differently.

Resources

Jordan, D. (n.d.) *Functional Behavioral Assessment and Positive Interventions: What Parents Need to Know* by Dixie Jordan. Retrieved from www.wrightslaw.com/info/discipl.fba.jordan.pdf

Center for Effective Collaboration and Practice. *An IEP Team's Introduction to Functional Behavioral Assessment and Behavior Intervention Plans.* Retrieved from cecp.air.org/fba/problembehavior/funcanal.pdf

New Mexico Public Education Department Technical Assistance Manual: Addressing Student Behavior. *Functional Behavior Assessments.* Retrieved from www.ped.state.nm.us/Rtl/behavior/4.fba.11.28.pdf

In Summation

In this chapter, you learned about adaptive behavior assessments and functional behavior assessments.

Let's move on to the next chapter where we will learn about transition assessments.

Endnotes

1. Sparrow, S., Cicchetti, D., & Balla, D. (2005). *Vineland Adaptive Behavior Scales, Second Edition (Vineland™-II)*. San Antonio, TX: Pearson. Retrieved from www.pearsonclinical.com/psychology/products/100000668/vineland-adaptive-behavior-scales-second-edition-vineland-ii-vinelandii.html#details

14 Transition Assessments

- Types of Transition Assessments

- Planning the Transition Assessment

- Tests and Inventories for Transition

- Answers to Questions about Transition Assessments

If you are like most parents, you worry about the future. Will your child have the knowledge and skills he needs when he leaves school? How can you ensure that he is prepared to get a job or go to college, live independently, and participate in the community? Transition assessments are a step to helping your child set goals for the future.

All About Tests and Assessments

Many parents and teachers are not aware that the Individuals with Disabilities Education Act (IDEA) requires schools to help children with disabilities during transitions. When your child makes the transition from early intervention services at age three, the child's team must develop a plan to ensure a smooth transition to the preschool program.[1]

Before your child turns 16, the IEP team must include measurable transition goals in her IEP. Some states require transition assessments, goals, and services by age 14.[2] These goals must be based on age-appropriate transition assessments.

Your child's IEP must include transition services, including courses of study, to help your child make a smooth transition to life after school.[3] Your child's team must update transition services annually.

Types of Transition Assessments

What are transition assessments? How are these assessments used?

Transition assessments identify your child's unique interests, strengths, preferences, and priorities for adult living.

Transition assessments are formal and informal. Formal assessments are standardized tests that have data showing that they are reliable and valid. Informal assessments are subjective. Examples of informal assessments are paper/pencil tests, observations, interviews, and functional skill inventories.

Transition experts recommend using standardized tests to confirm subjective information obtained from informal assessments.[4] Decisions about appropriate tests should be based on the child's unique needs.

Transition assessments may include:

- General and specific aptitude tests
- Adaptive behavior assessments
- Interest and work values inventories
- Intelligence tests and academic achievement tests
- Personality and preferences tests
- Work-related temperament scales
- Career maturity or readiness tests
- Self-determination assessments
- Transition planning inventories [5]

How old should my daughter be when we start the transition assessment process?

Your child's transition is an ongoing process that should begin when your child is in elementary school or middle school. The school must use age-appropriate transition assessments to create measurable transition goals for the IEP in effect before your daughter turns 16. Some states require transition assessments and goals by age 14.[6]

Who conducts transition assessments?

Many people are involved in transition assessments, including:

- Teachers and paraprofessionals who work with your child

- Speech and language pathologists, physical therapists, and school nurses

- Counselors, social workers, and psychologists [7]

Transition Services May Include:

- College and continuing education

- Vocational education

- Independent living and community participation

- Courses of study and advanced placement courses to prepare for future education

---

As a parent, do I have a role in the transition assessment process?

Yes. You have a unique perspective about your child. You can answer questions like these:

- What paid or non-paid work does my child enjoy and do well?

- What work-related skills has my child developed?

- Does my child participate in social groups with non-disabled children?

When you share information about your child with the team, you help the team select appropriate tests for the transition assessment. The right tests will provide information that is needed to create a good transition plan.

Your child needs to be involved in the transition assessment process too. Encourage her to think about her strengths, interests, and preferences.

Planning the Transition Assessment

Your child's IEP team should select tests and assessments to clarify your child's interests, strengths, preferences, and priorities for adult living.

What tests should be included in my child's transition assessment?

Each child is different so there are no required tests that must be included in a transition assessment. Think about your child's knowledge and skills in areas like these:

- Career awareness, workplace readiness, job-seeking strategies

- College and vocational education

- House, food, clothing, health, physical care

You and her school team need to consider her adaptive behavior and self-determination skills, including her skills in:

- Goal setting

- Problem solving

- Self-advocacy

- Independence and daily living skills

- Communication and social skills

- Technology

- Speaking and listening

- Math, money and finance

- Housing, food, clothing, and health,

- Transportation

Tests and Inventories for Transition

Thousands of tests and inventories are available for use in transition assessments. (See **Resources** at the end of this chapter.) Formal assessments include standardized tests of specific skills. Achievement tests measure your child's academic skills. See Chapters 5-8 for information about academic achievement assessments.

Adaptive behavior and independent living tests focus on your child's ability to live independently as a young adult.

The *Street Survival Skills Questionnaire (SSSQ)* measures adaptive behavior. The *SSSQ* is used to assess communication and basic living skills. Test items are designed to resemble everyday living skills. When used with an older adolescent, the *SSSQ* can measure the child's ability to live independently in the community and levels of vocational placement.

The *BRIGANCE® Transition Skills Inventory (TSI)* is a criterion-referenced assessment that measures a variety of transition skills including:

- Functional reading and writing

- Career awareness and job-seeking

A transition assessment is likely to include informal assessments that identify your child's strengths and needs. The *Enderle-Severson Transition Rating Scales (ESTR)* are informal assessments used to gather information about employment, recreation and leisure, home living, community participation, and post-secondary education.

The *ESTR* has different versions for students with mild disabilities and those with severe/multiple impairments. Parent questionnaires are provided in English and Spanish. Reports can be generated online.

Answers to Questions about Transition Assessments

My child does not read. Can any transition assessments be used with non-readers?

There are transition assessments that do not require reading skills. The *COPS Picture Interest Inventory (COPS-PIC)* is a nonverbal assessment of occupational interests that provides job interest scores in 14 career clusters. It is appropriate for children in grades 7-12, college, and beyond.

The *Reading-Free Vocational Interest Inventory (R-FVII)* uses pictures of individuals in different occupations to measure the preferences of individuals who are intellectually disabled and/or learning disabled.

It is probably not too late, however, to teach your child how to read. Reading is an essential life skill. If your child has weak reading skills, request a reading assessment as part of the transition assessment.

The school team does not want to do a transition assessment on my child because she is severely handicapped. What should I do?

You should insist that the school complete a comprehensive transition assessment on your child. The law does not create an exemption from the requirement to do transition assessments when a child has a severe disability.

Do not assume that a transition assessment will not be useful. Your daughter has unique needs that will be determined by transition assessments (e.g., education, training, employment, independent living skills).

In Summation

In this chapter, you learned about the requirements for transition assessments.

In the next chapter, you will learn about assessing children who are English Language Learners (ELLs) or who have limited English proficiency.

Resources

Disability Law Center. (2012) *Planning for Life After Special Education, Second edition.* Retrieved from www.dlc-ma.org/manual/

Kellems, R., and Morningstar, M.E. (June 2009) *Tips for Transition.* Retrieved from www.transitioncoalition.org/transition/tcfiles/files/docs/Tips_Nov09_final1258398594.pdf/Tips_Nov09_final.pdf

Walker, A.R., Kortering, L. J., Fowler, C.H., Rowe, D., & Bethune, L. (2013). *Age Appropriate Transition Assessment Toolkit, Third Edition.* Charlotte, NC: University of North Carolina. Retrieved from www.nsttac.org/content/age-appropriate-transition-assessment-toolkit-3rd-edition

Transition Coalition. Website provides online information, support, and professional development on topics about the transition from school to adult life for youth with disabilities. www.transitioncoalition.org/transition/

Transition, Transition Services, and Transition Planning: www.wrightslaw.com/info/trans.index.htm

College, Continuing and Higher Education: www.wrightslaw.com/info/college.index.htm

Endnotes

1. 20 U.S.C. §1412(a)(9); 20 U.S.C. §1436(a)(3) 34 C.F.R. §303.209; 34 C.F.R. §303.344

2. 34 C.F.R. §300.320

3. 20 U.S.C. §1414(d)(1)(A) and §1414(d)(6), 34 C.F.R. §320(b)

4. Clark, G. (2007). *Ask the expert: Transition assessment in transition planning.* Retrieved from http://transitionresponse.com/wp-content/uploads/2011/11/2011-11-14-Expert-Gary-Clark.pdf

5. National Secondary Transition Technical Assistance Center. (2013). *Age Appropriate Transition Assessment Toolkit, Third Edition.* Charlotte, NC: University of North Carolina. Retrieved from http://nsttac.org/content/age-appropriate-transition-assessment-toolkit-3rd-edition - section2B

6. Ibid

7. Transition Assessments Supplement. (December, 2012). In *Planning for Life After Special Education, 2nd Edition.* (p.96-103). Retrieved from www.dlc-ma.org/manual

15 Assessing English Language Learners (ELLs)

- Evaluating Children with Limited English Proficiency

- English Proficiency or Learning Disability?

- Tests for English Language Learners

- Assessing Reading in English Language Learners

- Assessing English Language Learners: Special Factors

- Internationally Adopted Children

Many children do not speak English as their native language. These children and their families have different cultural traditions and practices. This diversity brings new challenges to educators and evaluators.

Appropriate tests to assess culturally diverse English Language Learners (ELLs) are scarce. When an evaluator assesses a child who is learning English, she must know what the tests measure. Are the tests measuring the effect of limited English-language proficiency or the child's true skills?

In this chapter, you will learn why assessing children who are becoming proficient in English requires special expertise.

All About Tests and Assessments

You will learn that evaluators must distinguish between English Language Learner (ELL) and learning disability issues. This chapter will also explore how multicultural factors affect assessments.

Evaluating Children with Limited English Proficiency

Tests for English Language Learners must measure the skills they are supposed to measure, not the child's limited skills in the English language.

Who are English Language Learners?

Any child who is learning the English language in addition to her own native language is an English Language Learner or ELL.

ELL children have unique needs. An ELL child may have a disability that is masked by her difficulties with communicating in English. Schools must address the needs of ELLs so these children can benefit from their education.

Who should evaluate an English Language Learner?

An English Language Learner should be assessed in her native language (L1) by a bilingual evaluator. The bilingual evaluator should be fluent in the child's L1 and in English.

An evaluator who assesses ELLs must be knowledgeable about how a child acquires a second language (L2) and what it is like to adapt to a new culture. The evaluator needs to know how to conduct an assessment that is free of linguistic and cultural bias.

Should the evaluator assess an ELL child in her native language or with tests in English?

An ELL should be tested in her native language. The tests selected should be reliable, valid, and normed in both languages. The law requires that tests and evaluation materials be selected, provided, and administered in the child's native language "unless it is clearly not feasible to do so."[1]

The evaluator should examine the child's developmental milestones of early language. Difficulty acquiring the first language is a risk factor for acquiring a second.[2]

Table 15-1. Assessments of English Language Learners (ELLs)

- Background history of the child
- Family history
- Language proficiency and use of language in the home and in the community
- Socio-economic status
- Developmental milestones in native language (L1)
- Academic history including reading and writing skills in L1
- Curriculum-based data and observations
- Assessment of school's capacity to educate ELLs and multicultural learners (MCLs)
- Work Samples
- Intervention Results

English Proficiency or Learning Disability?

Most teachers do not have the training to distinguish between ELL issues and learning disabilities.[3] These teachers are unlikely to recognize the differences between conversational skills and the language needed to do well in school. A child may only be diagnosed with a language learning disability if she demonstrates difficulty in all languages.

My child is learning English (ELL). She is struggling in school. Could she have a language learning disability?

If your child acquired her first language (L1) easily, she does not have a language learning disability. If you believe that your child had difficulty acquiring her first language (L1), request an evaluation by the school.

The evaluator needs to review your child's background history to determine how her first language developed. The evaluator should collect language samples from home and school.

You should expect your child to go through stages before she is proficient in English. First, she will learn Basic Interpersonal Communication Skills (BICS). BICS is the language she will use to communicate with friends and in the community, but BICS is not sufficient to do well academically.

Listening, reading, and writing in school require a higher level of language skill than BICS. This higher language skill is Cognitive Academic Language Proficiency or CALP.

As a rule, it may take two years to be proficient in BICS and five to seven years to be proficient in CALP.[4]

When your child is acquiring English, it will take her longer to accomplish tasks in English. She may need accommodations including additional time on assignments and tests.[5] When your child has mastered English, she will have a good vocabulary and a strong command of sentence structure.

The school psychologist evaluated our ELL daughter. The intelligence test included tests of her vocabulary and verbal reasoning. He said her IQ was low. We do not agree. What should we do?

It is not appropriate to administer verbal tests of intellectual functioning to ELLs who are learning English language skills and background knowledge. You need to get an evaluation of your child's language proficiency.

Table 15-2. Behaviors of English Language Learners (ELLs) that Mimic Learning Disorders

- Inattention and distractibility
- Impulsivity and hyperactivity
- Forgetfulness and disorganization
- Disorganization and disruptiveness
- Reduced work rate

From *Best practices in Nondiscriminatory Assessment* by S. Ortiz.[6]

All About Tests and Assessments

I teach in a district with many ELL children. Their parents have limited skills in English. What are our responsibilities to parents who attend IEP meetings but do not understand English?

The parental participation section of the IDEA requires school districts to ensure that parents understand what is happening during IEP meetings. The school is required to provide an interpreter to parents whose native language is not English, and to parents who are deaf or hard of hearing.[7]

The school **must** inform parents of their right to an interpreter **before** IEP meetings.

The administrators at my school say they do not have access to interpreters. Are there resources outside the district that can provide interpreters?

The school district is **required** to provide interpreters. The district can contract with bilingual evaluators, as needed. The National Association of School Psychologists maintains an online list of bilingual evaluators.[8]

Tests Designed for English Language Learners

Few tests are available to measure the skills of ELLs. Can an evaluator use tests that were standardized on English-speaking children?

Sorry, no. Using tests that are standardized on children who speak English creates a host of problems.

- *Content bias* presumes that the student had access to language and cultural experiences in English.

- *Linguistic bias* presumes a match between the language of the examiner, the child, and the test. A child who speaks a different language may be penalized for language differences, not her weaknesses in articulation or grammar.

- *Norming samples* are children who were born and educated in the U.S. More than 300 languages are spoken in the U.S. The norming sample would have to account for the different ages at which children began to speak English.

Any standardized, norm-referenced test is likely to be biased toward children who were raised in the U. S.

Why can't normed, standardized tests be translated into other languages?

When you translate a test, you introduce *interpreter bias*. If the interpreter inadvertently changes the way test items are presented, the test is not standardized.

Assessing Reading in English Language Learners (ELLs)

Early reading skills do not depend solely on English-language skills. English language learners in kindergarten and first grade should be screened for weaknesses in phonological awareness.[9] This screening can be in English. Phonological awareness skills transfer from one language to another.[10]

Table 15-3. Tests That Assess the Skills of English Language Learners

Test	Description
Bateria-III Woodcock-Munoz NU (Bateria III)	Two batteries measure intellectual ability (including bilingual and low verbal), specific cognitive abilities, scholastic aptitude, oral language, and academic achievement in Spanish, ages 2-90+.
Bilingual Verbal Ability Test NU (BVAT)	Norm-referenced measure of vocabulary in 17 languages and English for bilingual individuals, ages 5 to 90+.
Boehm Test of Basic Concepts, 3rd Edition (Boehm-3)	Evaluates basic concepts necessary for school success in grades K-2. Directions provided in English and in Spanish.
Diagnostic Evaluation of Language Variation (DELV)	Assesses children who speak dialects other than American English. Provides a Language Variation Status for children ages 4-12 and a Diagnostic Risk Status for children ages 4-9.
Early Language Listening and Oral Proficiency Assessment (ELLOPA)	Language proficiency assessment; measures oral fluency, grammar, vocabulary, and listening comprehension for pre-K through grade 2.
Indicadores Dinamicos del Exito en la Lectura (IDEL)	Formative assessment series designed to measure the acquisition of basic early literacy skills in Spanish for grades K through 3.
Lindamood Auditory Conceptualization Test, 3rd Edition (LAC-3)	Measures phonological awareness and can be administered in Spanish and English for ages 5-18.
Preschool Language Scale, 4th Edition (PLS-4)	Measures auditory comprehension and expressive communication in bilingual children from birth through age 7.
Spanish Assessment of Basic Education, 2nd Edition (SABE/2)	Nationally-normed achievement test designed for Spanish speaking students in bilingual classrooms.
Test of Phonological Awareness in Spanish (TPAS)	Measures phonological awareness in Spanish speaking children ages 4 through 10.
Test de Vocabulario en Imagenes Peabody (TVIP)	A measure of Spanish receptive vocabulary for ages 2-6 through 17, based on the Peabody Picture Vocabulary Test in English.
Woodcock-Munoz Language Survey-Revised NU (WMLS-R NU	Norm-referenced test of reading, writing, listening, and comprehension for ages 2 through 90+; assesses language proficiency in English or Spanish..

Differences between the child's reading and listening skills can clarify the nature of the child's problem. If the child's reading and listening skills are poor, then reading comprehension problems are probably caused by ELL issues. If the child's listening skills are stronger than his reading, he is likely to have poor word recognition skills.

My child is learning to speak English. She did not learn to read well in Spanish. I worry that she will have trouble learning to read in English.

A background history will provide information about your child's acquisition of both languages - L1 and L2. Informal assessments focus on what your child is learning in the classroom. Formal measures include standardized, norm-referenced tests.

Some researchers recommend that evaluators use tests that measure short-term and working memory and phonemic awareness.[11] If the child has weaknesses in these areas, it is harder to learn.

Recording and transcribing language samples is helpful.

Assessing English Language Learners: Special Factors

How do multicultural factors affect testing?

Cultures have different rules that govern how people communicate. There are rules for how children and adults interact, make eye contact, respect personal space, think about

time, and even make small talk. In some cultures, learning problems are shameful.[12]

Evaluators who work with these children must be knowledgeable about social norms so they can discern the difference between a language disorder and a language difference. An evaluator who does not understand these rules is at risk for misdiagnosing a child who is acting according to the rules of his culture.

How does bilingualism affect the evaluations of ELLs?

A bilingual child can speak, listen, read, and write in two languages with age appropriate skills. A bilingual child can be evaluated in English. A five-year-old bilingual child should be able to speak and understand as well as other five-year-olds.[13]

Internationally Adopted Children

What should an evaluation of an internationally adopted (IA) child from an institution include?

An internationally adopted (IA) child from an institution should be evaluated by a process called "dynamic assessment."[14]

Dynamic assessment uses a "test-intervene-test" format to determine how the child learns. This format includes three steps. First, the examiner uses tests to establish a baseline. Second, the educator teaches. Third, the examiner retests the child and documents what the child learned.

Internationally adopted (IA) children have unusual backgrounds.

A comprehensive evaluation of an IA child should include:

- Reviews of medical records and reports from the country of origin.

- Interviews with parents and teachers using a behavioral inventory such as the *Vineland Adaptive Behavior Scales, Second Edition.* The inventory should not be used as a norm-referenced test.

- An assessment of language proficiency in the child's native language or English.

- A nonverbal intelligence test.

- An inventory of the child's academic and functional skills. The *Brigance Diagnostic Inventory* series assesses skills needed at school, at home, and in the community.

- An assessment of the child's behavioral and emotional functioning that uses behavior scales, clinical interviews, and teacher/parent observations.

We adopted a child from an orphanage in another country. The school says we should defer testing until our child settles in and learns some English. Is this correct?

No, this is not correct. Your child's native language skills should be evaluated as soon as possible.[15]

International adoptees (IAs) lose their native language skills at a surprisingly fast rate. A six-year-old will lose most of his expressive language skill within three months.

A nine-year-old will lose most of his native language within a year.

If IA children are not evaluated promptly, it may be impossible to determine their true native language skills.

We adopted a child from a Russian orphanage. The school psychologist who will evaluate our child is not a bilingual specialist. He wants a person who speaks Russian to help him with the assessment. Is this a good idea?

No. Evaluators of IA children from institutions require special expertise. In addition to knowledge about bilingual assessment, they need to know about the effects of neglect and abuse on child development.

We adopted our son from Poland a year ago. He does not remember a word of Polish. English is his only language. The school insists on doing a bilingual assessment. What should we do?

Your IA child is not bilingual.[16] A bilingual child does not speak two languages. When an IA child comes to the U. S., he stops speaking in his native language. His native language skills atrophy as the process of acquiring a new language begins.

It will take your child longer to learn English than to lose his first language. In educational jargon, bilingualism is an "additive" process that enhances the child's skills. For an IA child, the process is "subtractive" because the rate at which they acquire English is so slow.

An evaluation of a multicultural and multilingual learner must consider several variables, including the child's:

- Educational history

- Grade

- Proficiency in L1 and in L2[17]

In Summation

In this chapter, you learned about assessments that are appropriate to use with a bilingual child or an English Language Learner. You learned about the role of timing and other considerations when evaluating an internationally adopted child, including foreign language issues.

Endnotes

1. 20 U.S.C. §1412(a)(6)

2. Willig, A. (1986). Special education and the culturally and linguistically different child: An overview of issues and challenges. *Reading, Writing, and Learning Disabilities*, 2, 161-173

3. Cummins, J. (1984). *Bilingualism and special education: Issues in assessment and pedagogy.* San Diego, CA: College-Hill

4. Cummins, J. (1992). Language proficiency, bilingualism and academic achievement. In P. Richard-Amato, & M. Snow (Eds.), *The multicultural classroom: Readings for content-area teachers* (pp.16-26). White Plains, NY: Longman. Retrieved from http://web.pdx.edu/~fischerw/courses/advanced/methods_docs/pdf_doc/wbf_collection/0851-0900/0854_Cummins_profBilingAcad.pdf

5. Pitoniak, M., Young, J., Martiniello, M., King, T., Buteux, A., & Ginsburgh, M. (2009). *Guidelines for the assessment of English language learners* (p.14). Princeton, NJ: Educational Testing Service. Retrieved from www.ets.org/s/about/pdf/ell_guidelines.pdf

6. Ortiz, S. (2008). Best practices in nondiscriminatory assessment. In A. Thomas & J. Grimes (Eds.), *Best practices in school psychology* V (pp. 661-678). Bethesda, MD: National Association of School Psychologists

7. 34 C.F.R. §300.322(e)

8. NASP Directory of Bilingual Evaluators. Retrieved from www.nasponline.org/about_nasp/bilingualdirectory.aspx

9. Geva, E. (2000). Issues in the assessment of reading disabilities in L2 children – beliefs and research evidence. *Dyslexia*, 6, 13-28

10. Cisero, C. & Royer, J. (1995). The development and cross-language transfer of phonological awareness. *Contemporary Educational Psychology*, 20, 275-303

11. Laing, S., & Kamhi, A. (2003). Alternative assessment of language and literacy in culturally and linguistically diverse populations. *Language, Speech, and Hearing Services in Schools*, 34, 44-55

12. Sattler, J.M. & Hoge, R.D. (2006). *Assessment of children: Behavioral, social and clinical foundations* (5th Ed.), San Diego, CA: Jerome M. Sattler, Inc.

13. Gindis, B. (1998). Navigating uncharted waters: school psychologists working with internationally adopted post-institutionalized children. *Communiqué,* September 27(1), 6-9 and October 27(2), 20-23

14. Lidz, C. (1997). Dynamic assessment: Restructuring the role of school psychologists, *Communiqué*, 25(8), 22-23

15. Gindis, B. (n.d.) *Bilingual speech and language assessment.* Retrieved from www.bgcenter.com/BGCenterServices/SpeechandLanguage.htm

16. Gindis, B. (1998)

17. Rhodes, R., Ochoa, S., & Ortiz, S. (2005). *Assessing culturally and linguistically diverse students: A practical guide.* New York, NY: Guilford Press

Appendix: Table of Tests

Key: Test name, author, publisher, publisher website, age range, type of test.

Test Name, Author, Publisher	Age Range	Test Type
Adaptive Behavior Assessment System – Second Edition (ABAS®II, Harrison& Oakland, 2003, Pearson). www.pearsonclinical.com	Birth through 89	Functional Performance
AIMSweb (2001, Edformation). www.pearsonassessment.com	K through 8	Progress Monitoring
Alloway Working Memory Assessment-Second Edition (AWMA-2; Alloway, 2013, Pearson). www.pearsonclinical.com	5 through 79	Specialized – Memory
Assessment of Basic Language and Learning Skills-Revised (ABLLS-R; Partington, 2006, Behavior Analysts, Inc.). www.partingtonbehavioranalysts.com	Pre-K through 12.	Language & Functional Performance
Assessment of Literacy and Language (ALL; Lombardino, Lieberman, & Brown, 2005, Pearson). www.pearsonclinical.com	Pre-School through grade 1	Early Reading and Language
Bateria-III (Woodcock, Munoz-Sandoval, McGrew, & Mather, 2004, 2007, Riverside Publishing). www.riverpub.com	2 through 90+	Cognitive Achievement
Beery Buktenica Test of Visual-Motor Integration, Sixth Edition (BEERY™ VMI, Beery, Buktenica, & Beery, 2010, Pearson). www.pearsonassessment.com	2 through 100	Specialized – Visual & Motor
Bilingual Verbal Ability Test NU (BVAT; Munoz-Sandoval, Cummins, Alvarado, & Ruef, 1998 Riverside Publishing). www.riverpub.com	5 through 90+	Cognitive
Boehm Test of Basic Concepts, Third Edition (BOEHM-3; Boehm, 2000, Pearson). www.pearsonassessment.com	K through 2	Basic Academic Concepts
Brigance Diagnostic Inventory Series (Curriculum Associates). www.curriculumassociates.com	Birth through Adult	Achievement and Functional Performance

All About Tests and Assessments

Brigance Transition Skills Inventory (TSI; 2010, Curriculum Associates). www.curriculumassociates.com	Transition	Post Secondary Skills
Bruininks-Oseretsky Test of Motor Proficiency, Second Edition (BOT-2, Bruininks & Bruininks, 2005, AGS Inc). www.pearsonassessment.com	4 through 21	Specialized- Motor
Clinical Evaluation of Language Fundamentals, Fifth Edition (CELF-5; Semel, Wiig, & Secord, 2013, Pearson). www.pearsonassessment.com	5 through 21	Language
Comprehensive Assessment of Spoken Language (CASL; Carrow-Woolfolk, 1999, AGS Inc). www.pearsonassessment.com	3 through 21	Language
Comprehensive Mathematical Abilities Test (CMAT: Hresko, Schlieve, Herron, Swain, & Sherbenou, 2002, Pro-Ed). www.proedinc.com	7 through 18	Achievement
Comprehensive Receptive Expressive Vocabulary Test, Second Edition (CREVT-2; Wallace & Hammill, 2002, Pro-Ed). www.proedinc.com	4 through 89	Language
Comprehensive Test of Nonverbal Intelligence, Second Edition (CTONI-2; Hammill, Pearson, & Wiederholt, 2009, Pearson). www.pearsonassessment.com	6 through 89+	Cognitive Abilities
Comprehensive Test of Phonological Processing, Second Edition (CTOPP-2; Wagner, Torgesen, Rashotte, & Pearson 2013, Pro-Ed). www.proedinc.com	4 through 24	Specialized- Reading
COPS Picture Interest Inventory (COPS-PIC; Career Life Skills Resources, Inc.). www.career-lifeskills.com	Elementary through High School	Interest Inventory
Developmental Coordination Disorder Questionnaire-Revised 2007 (DCDQ 2007; Wilson & Crawford, Alberta Center for Child, Family and Community Research). www.dcdq.ca	5 through 15	Specialized Motor Skills
Developmental Test of Visual Perception – Third Edition (DTVP-3, Hammill, Pearson,& Voress, 2013, Western Psychological Services). www.wpspublish.com	4 through 12	Specialized – Visual
Diagnostic Assessment of Reading-Second Edition (DAR-2; Roswell, Chall, Curtis, & Kearns, 2005, Riverside). www.riverpub.com	5 to adult	Achievement

Diagnostic Evaluation of Articulation and Phonology (DEAP; Dodd, Hua, Crosbie, Holm, & Ozanne, 2006, PearsonPsychCorp). www.pearsonassessment.com	3 through 8	Language
Diagnostic Evaluation of Language Variation (DELV – Norm Referenced; Seymour, Roeper, de Villiers, with contributions by Peter A. de Villiers, 2005, Pearson). www.pearsonassessment.com	4 through 9	Language
Differential Ability Scales- Second Edition (DAS-II, Elliott, 2007, The Psychological Corp). www.pearsonclinical.com	2 through 17	Cognitive Abilities
Dynamic Inventory of Basic Early Literacy Skills – Sixth Edition (DIBELS; Good & Kaminski, 2007, Dynamic Measurement Group). www.dibels.org	K through 6	Early Achievement
Dynamic Inventory of Basic Early Literacy Skills Next (DIBELS-N; Good & Kaminski, 2010, Dynamic Measurement Group). www.dibels.org	K through 6	Progress Monitoring
Early Language Listening and Oral Proficiency Assessment (ELLOPA; 2001, Center for Applied Linguistics). www.cal.org/ela/sopaellopa/	Pre-K through 2	Language
Enderle-Severson Transition Rating Scale (ESTR,; 2005, Enderle & Severson, Estr Pub.). www.estr.net	Transition	Specialized Needs & Interests
Expressive One-Word Picture Vocabulary Test, Fourth Edition (EOWPVT-4; Martin & Brownell, 2011, Academic therapy Publications). www.academictherapy.com	2 through 80+	Language
Expressive Vocabulary Test, Second Edition (EVT-2; Williams, 2007, AGS Publishing). www.pearsonclinical.com	2-6 through 90+	Language
Functional Evaluation for Assistive Technology (FEAT; Raskind & Bryant, 2002, Psycho-Educational Services) www.psycho-educational.com	All ages	Specialized Technology
Goldman-Fristoe Test of Articulation, Second Edition (G-FTA-2; Goldman & Fristoe, 2000, American Guidance Service). www.pearsonschool.com	2 through 21	Language
Gray Diagnostic Reading Tests, Second Edition (GDRT-2; Bryant, Wiederholt, & Bryant, 2004, Pro-Ed). www.proedinc.com	6 through 13	Achievement
Gray Oral Reading Tests, Fifth Edition (GORT-5; Wiederholt & Bryant, 2012, Pro-Ed). www.proedinc.com	6 through 23	Achievement

All About Tests and Assessments

Gray Silent Reading Tests (GSRT, Wiederholt & Blalock, 2000, Pro-Ed). www.proedinc.com	7 through 25	Achievement
Illinois Test of Psycholinguistic Abilities, Third Edition (ITPA-3; Hammill, Mather, & Roberts, 2001, Pro-Ed). www.proedinc.com	5 through 12	Specialized Auditory
Indicadores Dinamicos del Exito en la Lectura (IDEL; Good III, Luft Baker, Knutson, & Watson, Eds. 2006, Dynamic Measurement Group). www.dibels.org	K through 3	Progress Monitoring
Informal Assessments for Transition Planning, Second Edition (Erickson, Clark, & Patton, 2012, Pro-Ed). www.proedinc.com	Transition	Inventory of Interests and Needs
Kaufman Speech Praxis Test for Children (KSPT; Kaufman, 1995, Wayne State University Press). www.wsupress.wayne.edu	2 through 5	Speech
Kaufman Test of Educational Achievement, Second Edition (KTEA-II; Kaufman & Kaufman, 2004, AGS Publishing). www.pearsonschool.com	4 through 25	Achievement
KeyMath Diagnostic Assessment, Third Edition (KeyMath3; Connolly, 2007, Pearson AGS). www.pearsonclinical.com	4-6 through 21	Achievement
Khan-Lewis Phonological Analysis, Second Edition (KLPA-2; Khan & Lewis, 2002, Pearson Clinical). www.pearsonclinical.com	2 through 21-11	Speech
Leiter International Performance Scale, Third Edition (Leiter-3; Roid, Miller, Pomplun, & Koch, 2013, Western Psychological Svcs). www.wpspublish.com	3 through 75+	Cognitive Ability
Lindamood Auditory Conceptualization Test, Third Edition (LAC-3; Lindamood & Lindamood, 2004, Gander Publishing). www.ganderpublishing.com	5 through 18	Specialized- Reading
Motor- Free Visual Perception Test, Third Edition (MVPT-3, Colarusso & Hammill, 2003, Academic Therapy Publications). www.academictherapy.com	4 through 70+	Specialized – Visual
Naglieri Nonverbal Ability Test, Second Edition (NNAT2; Naglieri, 2013, NCS Pearson). www.pearsonassessment.com	5 through 17	Cognitive Abilities

Oral and Written Language Scales, Second Edition (OWLS-II; Carrow-Woolfolk, 2011, Western Psychological Services). www.wpspublish.com LC= Listening comprehension RC= Reading comprehension OE= Oral expression WE= Written expression	LC and OE: 3-21 RC and WE: 5-21	Language and Achievement
Peabody Developmental Motor Scales, Second Edition (PDMS-2, Folio & Fewell, 2000, Riverside). www.riverpub.com	Birth through 5	Specialized – Motor
Peabody Picture Vocabulary Test, Fourth Edition (PPVT-4; Dunn & Dunn, 2007, Pearson). www.pearsonassessment.com	2-6 through 90+	Language
Phonological Awareness Test, Second Edition (PAT2; Robertson & Salter, 2007, Linguisystems). www.linguisystems.com	5 through 9	Specialized – Reading
Preschool Language Scale, Fourth Edition (PLS-4; Zimmerman, Steiner, & Evatt Pond, 2002, The Psychological Corporation). www.pearsonassessment.com	Birth through 6	Language
Primary Test of Nonvebal Intelligence (PTONI; Ehrler & McGhee, 2008, Pro-Ed). www.proedinc.com	3 through 9	Cognitive Abilities
Process Assessment of the Learner – Second Edition (PAL-II; Berninger, 2007, Pearson). www.pearsonassessment.com	K through 6	Specialized – Achievement
Reading-Free Vocational Interest Inventory: 2 (R-FVII:2; Becker, 2000, Elbern Publications). www.proedinc.com	14 through adult	Interest Inventory
Receptive One-Word Picture Vocabulary Test, Fourth Edition (ROWVT-4; Brownell (Ed.), 2010, Academic therapy Publications). www.academictherapy.com	Ages 2-0 through 70+	Language
Developmental Scoring System for the Rey-Osterrieth Complex Figure (DSS-ROCF; Bernstein & Waber, Psychological Assessment Resources, Inc.) www.parinc.com	Ages 5 to 14	Specialized: Spatial Organization
Spanish Assessment of Basic Education, Second Edition (SABE 2; CBT McGraw-Hill). www.ctb.com	Grades 2-11	Achievement
Standardized Reading Inventory, Second Edition (SRI-2; Newcomer, 1999, Pro-Ed). www.proedinc.com	6 through 14	Achievement

All About Tests and Assessments

Street Survival Skills Questionnaire (SSSQ; Linkenhoker & McCarron, 1993, McCarron-Dial Evaluation Systems). www.mccarrondial.com	9 through 40+	Independent and vocational Living Skills
Stuttering Prediction Instrument for Young Children (SPI; Riley, 1981, Pro-Ed). www.proedinc.com	3-8	Speech
Stuttering Severity Instruction, Fourth Edition (SSI-4; Riley, 2008, Pro-Ed). www.proedinc.com	2-10 and up	Speech
Test de Vocabulario en Imagenes Peabody (TVIP; Dunn(Lloyd), Hugo, Padilla, & Dunn(Liotta), 1986, Pearson). www.pearsonclinical.com	2 through 17	Language
Test of Adolescent and Adult Language, Fourth Edition (TOAL-4; Hammill, Brown, Larsen, Wiederholt, 2007, Pro-Ed). www.proedinc.com	12 through 24	Language
Test of Auditory Processing Skills, Third Edition (TAPS-3; Martin & Brownell, 2005, Western Psychological Services). www.wpspublish.com	4 through 18	Specialized – Auditory
Test of Early Mathematics Ability, Third Edition (TEMA-3; Ginsburg & Baroody, 2003, Pro-Ed). www.proedinc.com	3 through 8	Early Achievement
Test of Language Development Intermediate – Fourth Edition (TOLD-I:4; Hammill & Newcomer, 2008, Pro-Ed). www.proedinc.com	8 through 17	Language
Test of Language Development Primary – Fourth Edition (TOLD-P; Newcomer, Hammill, 2008, Pro-Ed). www.proedinc.com	4 through 8	Language
Test of Nonverbal Intelligence, Fourth Edition (TONI-4; Brown, Sherbenou, & Johnsen, 2010, Pro-Ed). www.proedinc.com	6 through 89	Cognitive Abilities
Test of Orthographic Competence (TOC; Mather, Roberts, Hammill, & Allen, 2008, Pro-Ed). www.proedinc.com	6 through 17	Specialized – Reading
Test of Phonological Awareness in Spanish (TPAS; Riccio, Imhoff, Hasbrouck, & Davis, 2004, Pro-Ed). www.proedinc.com	4 through 10	Specialized – Reading
Test of Phonological Awareness, Second Edition: Plus (TOPA-2+; Torgesen, & Bryant, 2004, Pro-Ed). www.proedinc.com	5 through 8	Specialized – Reading

Test of Pragmatic Language – Second Edition (TOPL-2; Phelps-Teraski, & Phelps-Gunn, 2007, Pro-Ed).www.proedinc.com	6 through 18	Language
Test of Reading Comprehension, Fourth Edition (TORC-4;Brown, Wiederholt, & Hammill, 2009, Pro-Ed). www.proedinc.com	7 through 17	Achievement
Test of Silent Contextual Reading Fluency (TOSCRF; Hammill, Lee, Wiederholt, & Allen, 2006, Pro-Ed). www.proedinc.com	7 through 18	Achievement
Test of Silent Word Reading Efficiency and Comprehension (TOSREC; Wagner, Torgesen, Rashotte, & Pearson, 2010, Pro-Ed). www.proedinc.com	Grades 1 through 12	Achievement
Test of Silent Word Reading Fluency (TOSWRF; Mather, Hammill, Allen, & Roberts, 2004, Pro-Ed). www.proedinc.com	6-6 through 17	Achievement
Test of Word Reading Efficiency, Second Edition (TOWRE-2; Torgesen, Wagner, & Rashotte, 2012, Pearson). www.pearsonassessment.com	6 through 24	Achievement
Test of Written Language, Fourth Edition (TOWL-4; Hammill & Larsen, 2009, Pro-Ed). www.proedinc.com	9 through 17	Achievement
Vineland Adaptive Behavior Scales, Second Edition (Vineland-II; Sparrow, Cicchetti, & Balla, 2005, American Guidance Services). www.pearsonschool.com	Birth through 90	Daily Living and Communication Skills
Wechsler Adult Intelligence Scale, Fourth Edition (WAIS-IV; Wechsler, 2008, Pearson). www.pearsonassessment.com	16 through 90	Cognitive Abilities
Wechsler Individual Achievement Test, Third Edition (WIAT-III; Wechsler, 2009, Pearson). www.pearsonassessment.com	4 through 50	Achievement
Wechsler Intelligence Scale for Children – Fourth Edition (WISC-IV; Wechsler, 2003, Pearson). www.pearsonassessment.com	6 through 16	Cognitive Abilities
Wechsler Preschool and Primary Scale of Intelligence, Fourth Edition (WPPSI-IV; Wechsler, 2012, Pearson). www.pearsonassessment.com	2 through 7	Cognitive Abilities

All About Tests and Assessments

Woodcock Reading Mastery Test, Third Edition (WRMT-3; Woodcock, 2011, Pearson). www.pearsonassessment.com	4 through 79	Achievement
Woodcock-Johnson III Normative Update (WJ III NU; Woodcock, Shrank, McGrew, & Mather, 2007, Riverside). www.riverpub.com	2 through 90+	Cognitive and Achievement
Woodcock-Johnson III Tests of Achievement (WJ III ACH; Woodcock, McGrew, & Mather, 2001, Riverside). www.riverpub.com	2 through 90+	Achievement
Woodcock-Johnson Tests of Cognitive Abilities (WJ III COG; Woodcock, McGrew, Mather, 2001, Riverside). www.riverpub.com	2 through 90+	Cognitive Abilities
Woodcock-Johnson-III Diagnostic Reading Battery (WJ III DRB; Woodcock, Mather, Shrank, 2007, Riverside). www.riverpub.com	2 through 80+	Achievement
Woodcock-Munoz Language Survey- Revised NU (Schrank, Wendling, Alvarado, & Woodcock, 2010, Riverside). www.riverpub.com	2 through 90+	Language
Word Identification and Spelling Test (WIST; Wilson & Felton, 2004, Pro-Ed). www.proedinc.com	7 through 18	Achievement
Working Memory Rating Scale (WMRS: Alloway, Gathercole, & Kirkwood, 2008, Pearson). www.pearsonassessment.com	5 through 11	Specialized – Memory

Glossary of Terms

Ability testing. Use of norm-referenced tests to evaluate an individual's performance in a specific area (i.e. cognitive, psychomotor, or physical functioning).

Achievement test. Norm-referenced test that measures competency in academic subject areas.

Adaptive behavior. The collective communication, daily living, and socialization skills that permit individuals to function with independence and dignity in their homes, schools, and communities.

Age equivalent. The chronological age in a population for which a score is the median (middle) score. If children who are 10 years and 6 months old have a median score of 17 on a test, the score 17 has an age equivalent of 10-6.

Age norms. Refers to the comparison between a child's performance on a test and other children of the same age in the norming sample that serves as the basis for the standard score.

Alternate assessment. Usually means an alternative to a paper and pencil test; refers to non-conventional, subjective methods of assessing achievement (e.g., work samples and portfolios).

Alternate form. Two or more versions of a test that are considered interchangeable in that they measure the same constructs in the same ways, are intended for the same purposes, and are administered using the same directions. Alternate forms are used when frequent administrations of a test might result in an increase of scores due to a practice effect; also known as equivalent form.

Aptitude tests. Tests that measure an individual's collective knowledge; often used to predict learning potential. See also ability test.

Articulation. The process by which the teeth, tongue, lips, and other speech organs make speech sounds.

Assessment. The process of testing students to identify and confirm skills and abilities as a foundation for educational decisions; often used interchangeably with evaluation.

Auditory processing disorder (APD). A developmental or acquired impairment that affects the ability to recognize, discriminate, integrate, order, and localize speech sounds; not the result of intelligence, language, or attention; also known as central auditory processing disorder (CAPD).

Automaticity. The ability to perform a task without conscious effort.

Average. The measure of central tendency. See mean, mode, and median.

Basal. A convention in testing that ensures that students do not spend too much time on items (skills) that are too easy for them. All items below the basal on a test are assumed to be correct and are awarded full credit.

All About Tests and Assessments

Behavior intervention plan. A plan of positive behavioral interventions in the IEP of a child whose behaviors interfere with his/her learning or that of others.

Bell curve. A term that refers to the bell shape of a normal distribution of scores in a population. The bell curve is symmetrical. Most individuals earn scores in the average range; there are equal numbers of individuals with exceptional skill and very low skill.

Benchmark. Levels of academic performance used as checkpoints to monitor progress toward academic goals and/or standards.

Bottom. Refers to lower-level items in a test. When a test has sufficient bottom, it is able to discriminate between lower levels of performance. The bottom of a test is particularly important when testing young children or children with poorly developed skills.

Ceiling. A rule for test administration that limits the time for testing and ensures that students will not struggle with items that are too difficult. When students reach the ceiling for a particular test or subtest, testing is stopped; items above the ceiling are not awarded credit.

Cognition. The study of how people think and solve problems.

Competency tests. Tests that measure proficiency in subjects like math and English. Some states require students to pass competency tests before graduating.

Composite score. The practice of combining two or more subtest scores to create one score that represents skills in an area. For example, a reading composite score may include an individual's scores on reading vocabulary and reading comprehension subtests.

Concrete thinking. A type of thought that focuses on observable, physical features and facts.

Confidence intervals. The range of scores that captures a student's true score with a degree of probability or confidence.

Correlation. A measure of the relationship between two or more variables (r).

Criterion-referenced test. A test that measures an individual's mastery of adefined body of knowledge, such as a weekly spelling lesson. The individual's performance is compared to an objective or performance standard, not to the performance of other students.
Criterion-referenced tests usually cover relatively small units of content and are closely related to instruction. Scores have meaning in terms of what the individual knows or can do, rather than in (or in addition to) their relation to the scores made by a norm group. Frequently, the meaning is given in terms of a cutoff score. Individuals who score above the cutoff are considered to have mastered the material, while those who score below the cutoff have not.

Curriculum-based assessment. A measurement of skill that is based on the content and methods used in the classroom. It is used to make specific determinations regarding a student's mastery of curriculum.

Curriculum-based measurement (CBM). A method of measuring student progress in academic areas including math, reading, writing, and spelling. The child is tested briefly (1 to 5 minutes) at frequent intervals (weekly, biweekly, monthly). The scores are recorded on a graph and compared to the expected performance on the content for that year. The graph allows the child's teacher and parents to see how the child's performance compares to expectations.

Decoding. The ability to apply the rules of phonics to words.

Derived score. A score obtained when raw scores are converted by numerical transformation (e.g., conversion of raw scores to percentile ranks or standard scores). Examples of derived scores are IQ scores, stanine scores, T scores, and z scores.

Diagnostic test. A test used to diagnose, analyze or identify specific areas of weakness and strength; to determine the nature of weaknesses or deficiencies; diagnostic achievement tests are used to measure skills.

Dysgraphia. An impairment in written language that is manifested in a profound challenge to the fine-motor skills needed for intelligible and efficient handwriting, and in basic grammar, spelling, sentence structure, and coherence. A diagnosis of dysgraphia presumes that the child has had appropriate opportunities to learn; it is not related to intelligence. Individuals with dysgraphia may be identified with a specific learning disability in written expression if the impairment adversely affects educational performance.

Dyslexia. A language-based learning disability that affects skill in reading. Individuals with dyslexia typically have difficulty with word recognition, fluency, and comprehension due to a weakness in phonological processing. These difficulties are not caused by poor instruction or limited intelligence. The term dyslexia appears in the definition of "specific learning disability."

Educational diagnostician. An individual who is trained and licensed to perform evaluations.

English language learner (ELL). A nonnative speaker of English who is acquiring English.

Equivalent form. See alternate form.

Executive functioning. The part of the brain that manages how individuals take in, store, and retrieve information.

Expressive language. The ability to express one's thoughts orally with grammar, precision, and style.

Fine motor skill. Small muscle movements that coordinate speech, handwriting, other activities requiring precision.

Floor. The lowest score that a test can reliably measure.

Fluency. The ability to read with speed, accuracy, intonation, and phrasing. Fluent reading is necessary for reading comprehension.

Fluid reasoning. The ability to use one's skills to solve novel problems.

Functional behavioral assessment (FBA). Strategies used to determine the underlying function or cause of a behavior so an effective intervention plan can be developed and implemented.

Grade equivalent. A way of describing test performance that is based on the average number of correct responses at a specific point in the school year in the norming sample. Use with caution.

Grade norms. Compares one student's score with the scores obtained by other students in the same grade on the same test. See also age norms.

Gross motor skill. Large muscle movements that coordinate skills such as walking and running.

Inferential thinking. The ability to draw conclusions and make connections within a text, and to make connections with one's background knowledge.

Informal evaluation. The measurement of knowledge or skill with teacher-made or nonstandardized tests.

Informal reading inventory (IRI). A type of reading test that consists of word lists and passages of increasing difficulty that provide levels of reading instruction (frustration, instructional, and independent). Some IRIs are teacher-made; others are published. IRIs that do not provide evidence of reliability and validity should not be used to make high-stakes decisions.

Intelligence. A controversial and illusive construct that attempts to define an individual's problem solving abilities or potential for learning.

Intelligence quotient (IQ). A statistic or score on a standardized test that attempts to quantify an individual's problem solving abilities and potential for learning.

Interscorer reliability. A measure that defines the degree to which two evaluators are able to arrive at the same score when following the instructions for test administration.

Limited English Proficient (LEP). A term that describes a nonnative speaker of English.

Long-term memory. A stage of memory that holds information for permanent access.

Mastery test. A test that determines whether an individual has mastered a unit of instruction or skill; a test that provides information about what an individual knows, not how his or her performance compares to a norm group.

Matthew Effects. A term coined by Keith Stanovich to describe the cognitive, behavioral, and motivational consequences that the slow aquisition of reading has on an individual; that these consequences slow the development of other cognitive skills and inhibit performance on many academic tasks.

Mean. A type of average; the sum of individual scores divided by the total number of scores. If Sam takes three tests, and he earns scores of 90, 96, and 99, his average score is 95.

Median. The middle score in a distribution of ranked scores; the median divides a group into two equal parts; the 50th percentile rank. If Sam takes three tests, and he earned scores of 85, 92, and 110, his median score is 92. Median scores are less subject to extremes in performance.

Mode. The score that occurs most often in a distribution.

Narrative writing. Writing that tells a story.

Neurology. The study of diseases that involve the central nervous system.

Neuropsychology. The study of the structure and function of the brain as related to psychological processes and behaviors.

Nonliteral language. Language in which the meaning is not directly stated.

Nonverbal. Without language, oral or written.

Nonverbal learning disability. A disorder in spatial thinking, gross motor and fine motor skills that affects the development of social skills, higher-level language skills, written expression, and math.

Nonverbal intelligence tests. Tests that are designed to permit individuals to demonstrate their abilities and problem solving skills through tasks that do not require language.

Normal distribution. A distribution of scores used to scale a test. A normal distribution curve is a bell-shaped curve with most scores in the middle and a small number of scores at the low and high ends.

Normative sample. A well-defined group of individuals who are selected to reflect the demographic characteristics (age, gender, grade, income, disability) of the population used to scale a test.

Norms. Refers to "normative sample." See age norms or grade norms.

Out-of-level testing. Refers to the practice of assessing students in one grade with tests designed for students in other (usually lower) grade levels; may not assess the same standards.

Percentiles (percentile rank). Percentage of scores that fall below a point on a score distribution; for example, a score at the 75th percentile indicates that 75% of students obtained that score or lower.

Perceptual reasoning. The ability to perceive relationships, recognize patterns, and draw conclusions based on abstract geometric designs and meaningful pictures.

Performance standards. Definitions of what a child must do to demonstrate proficiency at specific levels in content standards.

Phonemic awareness. An awareness of individual speech sounds in words.

Phonics. The study of how the sound patterns of language are represented by letter symbols.

Phonological awareness. An awareness of the sound patterns of oral language.

Portfolio assessment. A collection of work samples that provide evidence of progress and learning; can be designed to assess achievement and effort.

Power test. Measures performance unaffected by speed of response; time is not critical; items are usually arranged in order of increasing difficulty.

Probe. A brief test, typically 1 to 5 minutes in duration, that is used to measure progress on a frequent basis.

Processing deficits. Weaknesses in cognitive functioning that may compromise an individual's skill in academic tasks or problem solving.

Processing speed. The ability to make small decisions, often visual in nature, and to record them with a pencil while being timed.

Proficient. Solid academic performance for a grade, demonstrated competence in subject matter.

Progress monitoring. A scientifically based practice used to assess academic performance and evaluate the effectiveness of instruction; can be implemented with individuals or an entire class.

Protocol. The form provided by a test publisher that is used by an evaluator to record an individual's performance on a test.

Psychiatry. A branch of medicine that involves the study and treatment of mental disorders.

Psychology. The study of the mind, mental processes, and behaviors.

Rapid automatic naming (RAN). The ability to name pictured objects, colors, letters, and/or numbers while being timed. Some believe that rapid naming is a measure of executive functioning.

Raw score. The points earned by a student for correct responses on a test. Raw scores are converted to standard scores, percentile ranks, grade equivalents, and age equivalents.

Receptive language. The ability to understand language as it is used by others.

Reevaluation. An evaluation that is repeated after an agreed upon interval to determine present levels of functioning and progress.

Reliability. The consistency with which a test measures the areas being tested; describes the extent to which a test is dependable, stable, and consistent. There are different types of reliability: test-retest, internal consistency, and alternate form. For a test to be valid, it must provide results that are reliable.

Remediation. Process by which an individual receives instruction and practice in skills that are weak or nonexistent with the goal of developing/strengthening these skills.

Response to intervention (RTI). The use of research-based instruction with students who are risk and who are suspected of having specific learning disabilities; the degree to which students benefit (or fail to benefit) from changes in instruction that are designed to improve performance.

Scaled score. A type of standard score that has a range of 1 to 19, a mean of 10, and a standard deviation of 3.

Scientifically based research. Research that applies rigorous, systematic, and objective procedures to obtain reliable, valid knowledge about education activities and programs.

Score. A number that describes a level of skill that results from the administration of a test.

Screening. A brief assessment that may determine the need for further testing.

Sensory processing. The ability to take in information through one's senses: seeing, hearing, touching, tasting, and smelling.

Short-term memory. A temporary buffer zone where new learning is stored in memory for a few seconds.

Spatial processing. The ability to process what we see.

Standard deviation (SD). A measure of how scores spread out from the mean; the more scores cluster about the mean, the small the SD. If a scoring system has a mean of 100 and a standard deviation of plus or minus 15, then scores from 85 to 115 will capture about two-thirds of the population.

Standard error of measurement (SEM). A statistic provided by test publishers that describes the reliability or consistency of a test. Because no test is perfectly reliable, scores are interpreted with a plus or minus value, a standard error; SEM varies from test to test, from subtest to subtest, and by age/grade of the students tested.

Standard score (SS). This term has two meanings. A standard score on a norm-referenced test is based on the bell curve and its distribution of scores from the average or mean. Standard scores are useful because they allow comparison between students and comparisons of one student over time. A standard score may also refer to a scoring system with a mean of 100 and a standard deviation of 15.

Standardization. A process that ensures that test content and the rules for administering a test is clearly defined so all examiners administer the test in the same way. The purpose of standardization is to ensure that individuals are assessed under the same conditions.

Standardized test. A test that is uniformly developed, administered, and scored. The term is often used interchangeably with a norm-referenced test; all norm-referenced tests are standardized.

Standards. Statements that describe what students are expected to know and be able to do in each grade and subject area; includes content standards, performance standards, and benchmarks.

Stanine. A standard score with a range of 1 to 9, a mean of 5 and a standard deviation of 1.97.

Strength. An ability or skill that is above average and significantly better than the individual's other abilities.

Subtest. A part of a test that that measures a specific area such as word identification or reading comprehension.

T-score. A standard score with a mean of 50 and a standard deviation of 10.

Test. A collection of questions that may be divided into subtests that measure abilities in one area or in several areas.

Test bias. The difference in test scores that is attributable to demographic variables (e.g. gender, ethnicity, and age).

Test procedures. The rules for administering a test.

Test-retest reliability. The consistency of a test over repeated administrations.

All About Tests and Assessments

Testing-to-the-limits. The practice of administering additional test items or altering the standard rules for administration after the test is completed with the goal of gathering additional information about an individual's performance. Testing-to-the-limits provides qualitative information only.

Top. A term that refers to the more challenging or difficult items on a test. When a test has a sufficient top, it permits evaluators to distinguish between extremely high levels of functioning and merely high levels of functioning.

True score. The average score obtained by an individual if the test could be administered an infinite number of times.

Validity. The degree to which a test measures what it purports to measure, and the extent to which inferences and actions made on the basis of test scores are appropriate and accurate.

Verbal. Related to language.

Visual. That which can be seen by the eye.

Visual-motor. The ability to coordinate the hand with the eye.

Weakness. A below average score that stands out in contrast to better-developed skills.

Word attack. The application of phonics skills to words.

Word recognition. Identifying words that may or may not follow the rules of phonics.

Working memory. A cognitive workspace or blackboard where new learning is compared, contrasted, and integrated with background knowledge.

Z-score. A type of standard score with a mean of 0 and a standard deviation of 1.

Index

All About Tests and Assessments

All About Tests and Assessments